Beyond Right

CHAIRMAN
Rabbi Moshe Kotlarsky

PRINCIPAL BENEFACTOR
Mr. George Rohr

EXECUTIVE DIRECTOR
Rabbi Efraim Mintz

—

AUTHOR
Rabbi Shmuel Super

EDITOR
Rabbi Naftali Silberberg

ADVISORY BOARD
Rabbi Levi Dubov
Rabbi Shimon Posner
Rabbi Sholom Raichik
Mrs. Rivkah Slonim
Rabbi Avrohom Sternberg

Cover Art: *The Merchant,* Michoel Muchnik, 1990, mixed media, New York

718-221-6900
WWW.MYJLI.COM

Beyond Right

The values that shape
Judaism's civil code

The Rohr Jewish Learning Institute
gratefully acknowledges the pioneering
and ongoing support of

George and Pamela Rohr

Since its inception, the Rohr JLI has been
a beneficiary of the vision, generosity, care,
and concern of the Rohr family.

In the merit of the tens of thousands of hours
of Torah study by JLI students worldwide,
may they be blessed with health, *Yiddishe
nachas* from all their loved ones, and
extraordinary success in all their endeavors.

Citation Types

SCRIPTURE

The icon for Scripture is based on the images of a scroll and a spiral. The scroll is a literal reference; the spiral symbolizes Scripture's role as the singular source from which all subsequent Torah knowledge emanates.

SCRIPTURAL COMMENTARY

Throughout the ages, Jews scrutinized the Torah's text, generating many commentaries.

TALMUD AND MIDRASH

The Talmud and Midrash record the teachings of the sages—fundamental links in the unbroken chain of the Torah's transmission going back to Mount Sinai.

TALMUDIC COMMENTARY

The layers of Talmudic teaching have been rigorously excavated in each era, resulting in a library of insightful commentaries.

JEWISH MYSTICISM

The mystics explore the inner, esoteric depths. The icon for mystical texts reflects the *"sefirot* tree" commonly present in kabbalistic charts.

JEWISH PHILOSOPHY

Jewish philosophic texts shed light on life's big questions and demonstrate the relevance of Jewish teachings even as the sands of societal values continuously shift.

JEWISH LAW AND CUSTOM

The guidance that emerges from Scripture and the Talmud finds practical expression in Jewish law, known as *Halachah* ("the way"), alongside customs adopted by Jewish communities through the generations.

CHASIDUT

Chasidism's advent in the eighteenth century brought major, encouraging changes to Jewish life and outlook. Its teachings are akin to refreshing, life-sustaining waters from a continuously flowing well of the profoundest insights.

PERSPECTIVES

Personal, professional, and academic perspectives, expressed in essays, research papers, diaries, and other works, can often enhance appreciation for Torah ideas and the totality of the Jewish experience.

Contents

Foreword

THESE ARE THE THINGS YOU ARE TO DO: SPEAK TRUTH TO EACH OTHER,
AND RENDER TRUE AND PEACEFUL JUDGMENT IN YOUR COURTS.

—ZECHARIAH 8:16

It is not surprising to find the Jewish bookshelf stocked with tomes on the laws of Shabbat observance or Jewish dietary requirements. By contrast, many are astonished to discover the attention Jewish law devotes to disputes between neighbors, ethical dilemmas involving the workplace, and a vast corpus of civil legislation.

Each legal system reflects the values to which its formulators adhere. This is profoundly true of Jewish law, which views its mandate—beyond protecting individual rights and maintaining social order—as shaping a righteous society.

Jewish civil law is not simply a system historically developed by Jews, but an inherently *Jewish* institution that reflects and promotes a set of values that is uniquely Jewish—and historically remarkable and revolutionary. Study of Jewish civil law clarifies the meaning of core Jewish values, for it is the station at which ideals convert into concrete practice, in the form of instruction and guidance for daily life and its myriad experiences.

To this end, the Rohr Jewish Learning Institute (JLI) is pleased to present *Beyond Right*, a groundbreaking course that pursues six primary Jewish values from their conception in Hebrew Scripture through their development in the teachings of our ancient sages, and on through subsequent generations of classic works of Jewish philosophy and mysticism. Then, following an in-depth slice of Talmudic study, these values come alive in the practical application of Jewish civil legislation, translating abstract principles into detailed guidance on common real-life scenarios.

We are confident that this study will clarify the uniqueness of several of Judaism's values and generate an appreciation for Jewish law as a uniquely Jewish system that Jews should approach for guidance and clarity when faced with professional or personal dilemmas.

Endorsements

"Law is what we must do. Ethics is what we should do. Jewish law goes beyond the 'must' to deeply embed a sense of values—*tzedek*, or righteousness—into its very fabric. This differs in important ways from American law, which often focuses on rights rather than obligations. Understanding these nuances illuminates our legal and moral obligations, and the new comparative law course from Rohr Jewish Learning Institute offers a thoughtful introduction to these important differences."

PAUL ROOT WOLPE, PHD

Raymond F. Schinazi Distinguished Research Chair in Jewish Bioethics

Director, Center for Ethics
Emory University

"The word 'Talmudic' is often deployed today as a synonym for hair-splitting legalism. This book shows how very basic principles can guide specialized decisions—how the spirit of the law emerges in the details. There's a lot here to challenge and inspire anyone with an interest in legal decision-making—and a lot to nurture appreciation for Talmud."

JEREMY A. RABKIN, PHD

Professor of Law
Antonin Scalia Law School
George Mason University

Author, *Law without Nations?*

"From birth to death, humans depend on each other. . . . Judaism has adopted law, culture, and empathy in regulating Jews' relationships. Studying this system enriches our ability to live under different laws in cultures around the world, yet follow our own principles."

TAMAR FRANKEL, LLM

Professor of Law Emerita
Boston University School of Law

Author, *Fiduciary Law*, and nine other titles

"The Talmudic legal system was established thousands of years ago, but it could not be more relevant to us today. In some respects, it is the foundation of some of the bedrock concepts in the American legal system. In other respects, it is premised on values that may seem alien to our individualistic modern American society. Understanding both the overlaps and the stark contrasts between these two systems provides valuable insights into the essential elements of a legal system, and how it both shapes and reflects the civilization of which it is a part. This course helps shine a light on what it means to be a nation living under the rule of law, and indeed, what it means to be human."

MARTIN PRITIKIN, JD

Dean, Concord Law School
Purdue University

"The JLI course *Beyond Right* explores fundamental topics that are of vital importance for any just society in light of the profound teachings of the Jewish legal tradition, and it highlights the central values and commitments that are at stake in addressing these issues. I commend JLI for developing this rich and illuminating course."

DAVID FLATTO, PHD

Associate Professor
Faculty of Law and Department of Jewish Philosophy
Hebrew University of Jerusalem

"The concept of *Beyond Right* encompasses the message and lesson that the Halakhic tradition can convey to modern Western Law. In terms of legal theory, 'taking rights seriously' is not enough—what goes 'beyond rights' must also be taken seriously. The approach of the JLI course is that distinction between rights-based, duty-based, and goal-based jurisprudences is not exclusive but deserves to coalesce. Indeed, the lurking danger of rights-based legal systems is moral blindness to principles and values that are 'beyond rights.' [These values are necessary] for a just and responsible society and, mainly, openness to the inevitable need to balance rights and principles."

DAVID JOSEPH, ESQ.

Faculty of Law
Hebrew University of Jerusalem

Author, *The Family and the Political: On Belonging and Responsibility in a Liberal Society,* and other titles

"American law is centered on the idea that persons are born with rights which they assert against the state and each other. Jewish law, by contrast, is founded on the belief that its adherents are born into a setting of duty and obligation towards G-d and their community and thus offers a countermodel to the rights-centric assumptions of American law. This course opens with these grounding premises and proceeds to examine how each system approaches concrete questions that arise from the experience of living together. As the bonds of society continue to deteriorate, deeper consideration of a legal system grounded in obligations rather than rights may serve as a useful corrective."

CHAIM SAIMAN, JD

Professor of Law

Chair in Jewish Law
Charles Widger School of Law
Villanova University

Continuing Education Credits

FOR ATTORNEYS

The course

Beyond Right

has been approved in these states for fulfillment of the continuing education requirements for legal and ethics credits:

United States

Alabama	*Iowa*	*Oklahoma*
Alaska	*Kansas*	*Oregon* *
Arkansas	*Kentucky*	*Pennsylvania*
California	*Louisiana*	*Rhode Island*
Colorado	*Minnesota*	*South Carolina*
Connecticut	*Missouri*	*Tennessee*
Delaware	*Montana*	*Utah*
Florida	*Nevada*	*Virginia* *
Georgia	*New Jersey*	*Washington*
Idaho	*New York* *	*Wisconsin*
Illinois *	*North Carolina*	
Indiana	*Ohio* *	

*Pending approval at the time this book went to print

TZEDAKAH GIRL
Leah Raab, acrylic on canvas. A young girl gives charity to a needy man, illuminating the dark street.

BEYOND GOOD NEIGHBORS

Most laws are designed to protect the rights of people and their property. But Judaism's civil code is driven by a different goal: shaping an upright society. In this lesson we explore how this value guides Jewish law, establishing its attitude toward neighborly disputes and interpersonal ethical dilemmas.

I. THE PURPOSE OF LAW

Welcome to an exploration of the underlying values of Jewish law and the laws they shape.

In this course, we will explore what makes Jewish civil law "Jewish" and unique, and what this means to us living in a society governed by a secular, non-Jewish legal system.

This lesson focuses on the basic question of the purpose of law: Is the function of law merely regulating society to protect people's rights, or should it seek to shape society and promulgate righteous conduct? If law should promote righteous conduct, how far should it go in this regard? The way a legal system defines its purpose dictates what values it incorporates and how they are applied.

EXERCISE 1.1

If you were a referee given a few minutes to address the players before a game of football, what would be the top three things you would say?

1

2

3

If you were a coach given a few minutes to address the players before a game of football, what would be the top three things you would say?

1

2

3

Divide the words on the following list into two categories and give each category a descriptive title. If you wish, you can then add further examples for each category.

CATEGORY 1:	CATEGORY 2:

Teacher	Parent	Police officer
Coach	Referee	Rule book
Playbook	Government	G-d

TEXT 1

Secular Law

Marquis de Lafayette, et al., Declaration of the Rights of Man, adopted by National Assembly of France, August 26, 1789, Articles 4–5

Liberty consists in the freedom to do everything which injures no one else; hence the exercise of the natural rights of each man has no limits except those which assure to the other members of the society the enjoyment of the same rights. These limits can only be determined by law.

Law can only prohibit such actions as are hurtful to society. Nothing may be prevented which is not forbidden by law, and no one may be forced to do anything not provided for by law.

DECLARATION OF THE RIGHTS OF MAN

The Declaration of the Rights of Man and of the Citizen was adopted by France's National Constituent Assembly in 1789. Written by the Marquis de Lafayette in consultation with Thomas Jefferson, the Declaration defines the principles of individual and collective rights that inspired the French Revolution. The Declaration has influenced and inspired rights-based liberal democracy throughout the world.

First printed edition of the Declaration of the Rights of Man and of the Citizen, 1789 (National Library of France)

TEXT 2

The Why of Jewish Law

Rabbi Don Yitzchak Abarbanel, Exodus 21:1

אֵין קִבּוּץ בִּבְנֵי אָדָם שֶׁלֹּא יִהְיֶה בֵּינֵיהֶם מִשְׁפָּטִים . . .

וּמָה הַמַּעֲלָה הַזֹּאת לְמִשְׁפְּטֵי ה' אֱמֶת עַל . . .

מִשְׁפְּטֵי שְׁאָר הָאוּמוֹת שֶׁעֲלֵיהֶם נֶאֱמַר וְאֵלֶּה

הַמִּשְׁפָּטִים אֲשֶׁר תָּשִׂים לִפְנֵיהֶם כְּאִלּוּ הָיְתָה יְדִיעָה

הָעֶלְיוֹנָה נִתְּנָה הָאֱלֹקִים לָהֶם לְבַדָּם . . .

מִצַּד טֶבַע הַמִּשְׁפָּטִים עַצְמָם, שֶׁהָאֱלֹקִיִּים כּוֹלְלִים

דְּבָרִים אֲחָדִים מַה שֶּׁלֹּא יִמָּצְאוּ בְּמִשְׁפְּטֵי הָאוּמוֹת . . .

מִשְׁפְּטֵי ה' הֵם מְיֻסָּדִים עַל הָרַחֲמִים וְהַטּוֹב.

Every human society requires laws.... What is the advantage of G-d's* Torah laws over ... the legal systems set up by other nations? Why does the verse state that "these are the laws you shall set before them," thereby telling us that these laws are a unique divine system exclusively given to us by G-d? ...

The reason for this is that the divine laws contain elements absent from other legal systems.... G-d's laws are based on the principles of compassion and goodness.

RABBI DON YITZCHAK ABARBANEL 1437–1508

Biblical exegete and statesman. Abarbanel was born in Lisbon, Portugal, and served as a minister in the court of King Alfonso V of Portugal. After intrigues at court led to accusations against him, he fled to Spain, where he once again served as a counselor to royalty. It is claimed that Abarbanel offered King Ferdinand and Queen Isabella large sums of money for the revocation of their Edict of Expulsion of 1492, but to no avail. After the expulsion, he eventually settled in Italy, where he wrote a commentary on Scripture, as well as other venerated works.

---

* Throughout this book, "G-d" and "L-rd" are written with a hyphen instead of an "o" (both in our own translations and when quoting others). This is one way we accord reverence to the sacred divine name. This also reminds us that, even as we seek G-d, He transcends any human effort to describe His reality.

TEXT 3

"Right and Good"

Deuteronomy 6:17–18

שָׁמוֹר תִּשְׁמְרוּן אֶת מִצְוֺת ה' אֱלֹקֵיכֶם . . .
אֲשֶׁר צִוָּךְ. וְעָשִׂיתָ הַיָּשָׁר וְהַטּוֹב בְּעֵינֵי ה'.

Diligently observe G-d's commandments . . .
that He has commanded you. Do what
is right and good in G-d's eyes.

**A JEWISH SHOPKEEPER
WITH TWO CLIENTS**
Jan van Grevenbroeck
(1731–1807),
watercolor on paper
(Correr Museum, Venice, Italy)

TEXT 4

Law That Creates Life

Rabbi Yosef Yitzchak Schneersohn, cited in *Hayom Yom*, 22 Shevat

עֶס זַיִּינֶען דָא צְווֵיי עָרְלֵיי חוּקִים:

א) אַ גֶעזֶעץ וֶועלְכֶער שַׁאפְט לֶעבְּעֶן.

ב) אַ גֶעזֶעץ וֶועלְכֶער וֶוערְט בַּאשַׁאפְּען פוּן לֶעבְּעֶן.

מֶענְשְׁלִיכֶע גֶעזֶעצְעֶן זַיִּינֶען גֶעשַׁאפְּען פוּן לֶעבְּעֶן . . . תּוֹרַת
ה', אִיז דֶער גֶ-טְלִיכֶער גֶעזֶעץ וֶועלְכֶער שַׁאפְט אַ לֶעבְּעֶן.

There are two types of laws:

a) Laws that create life

b) Laws created by life

Human laws are created by life. . . . G-d's
Torah is a divine law that creates life.

RABBI YOSEF YITZCHAK SCHNEERSOHN (RAYATZ, FRIERDIKER REBBE, PREVIOUS REBBE) 1880–1950

Chasidic rebbe, prolific writer, and Jewish activist. Rabbi Yosef Yitzchak, the sixth leader of the Chabad movement, actively promoted Jewish religious practice in Soviet Russia and was arrested for these activities. After his release from prison and exile, he settled in Warsaw, Poland, from where he fled Nazi occupation and arrived in New York in 1940. Settling in Brooklyn, Rabbi Schneersohn worked to revitalize American Jewish life. His son-in-law Rabbi Menachem Mendel Schneerson succeeded him as the leader of the Chabad movement.

FAITH
Detail from an elaborately decorated 18th-century parchment manuscript of the Scroll of Esther. Richly painted miniatures depict the scenes of the Purim story, as well as related allegorical figures such as this one depicting a seated man holding an open book and a Torah scroll. The style of the art points to a northern Italian origin.

II. WHEN IS DOING THE RIGHT THING AN OBLIGATION?

We've established that Torah law seeks to shape society rather than just regulate it and maintain order. We begin this section with four case studies that raise the tension between personal rights and doing the right thing, and then proceed to explore the multiple ways in which practical Jewish law aims to shape the society it governs.

CASE STUDY A   Jake Rossen, "The Man Who Built a 40-Foot Spite Fence Around His Neighbor's Home," mentalfloss.com, April 24, 2017

> Nicholas Yung considered himself a lucky man. A German who immigrated to the United States in 1848, Yung had worked hard to carve out a living for himself and eventually prosper as the owner of a mortuary in San Francisco. The business allowed him and wife Rosina to purchase a modest lot on the top of California Street Hill, where they built a quaint, cottage-style home and planted a beautiful garden. Every day, California sunlight and fresh air would stream in through their windows.
>
> Yung had no reason to believe that anything could interrupt his idyllic life, or that any one person could somehow deprive him of the beautiful days he had worked so hard to enjoy. But Yung also hadn't accounted for Charles Crocker, a very rich and very petty man who would eventually become both his neighbor and the bane of his existence. . . .

At 6 feet tall and 300 pounds, Charles Crocker cut an imposing figure. He had filled his bank account by being one of the "Big Four" barons behind the building of the Central Pacific Railroad. By the 1870s, he could afford whatever he desired. And what he wanted was to loom over S. Francisco like a gargoyle.

Crocker and his wealthy partners began scouting California Street Hill for its scenic views and proximity to the city's financial district.... Soon a group of wealthy men, including Crocker, were buying up all the homes on their chosen blocks. By the time Crocker was finished, he had erected a 12,000-square-foot mansion. With its new, wealthy inhabitants, California Street Hill was renamed Nob Hill.

As the project neared completion in 1876, there was one nagging detail: On the northeast corner of the block, Nicholas Yung was reluctant to sell. His cottage was dwarfed by the mansions going up, but he had come to enjoy the neighborhood....

With one or both men causing acrimony, the end result was that Yung was not moving.... At a reported cost of $3,000, Crocker had his workers construct a wooden fence on his land that towered over three sides of Yung's home. With its 40-foot-tall panels, the enclosure acted like a window shade, blotting out the sun and cool air and immersing Yung in darkness.

Should Charles Crocker's fence be legally allowed to stand?

◯ Yes   ◯ No

An 1878 photograph of S. Francisco by Edward Muybridge shows the spite fence built by Charles Crocker, annotated by Bruce C. Cooper.

CASE STUDY B

Rachel maintains a large and beautiful flower bed in her yard. But one day her neighbor Joe built a high wooden fence between their properties that cast shade over the garden, causing the flowers to die. When Rachel asked Joe why his fence needed to be so high, she was told that it was necessary to protect his birds from cats entering the property. Rachel offered to replace the wooden fence with a glass screen at her personal expense, in order to allow her flowers to receive sunlight without exposing Joe's birds to danger. But Joe refused to allow Rachel to replace the fence, without offering any reason.

Should Joe be legally required to allow Rachel to replace his wooden fence with a glass screen?

Yes   No

CASE STUDY C

Michael moved into a new house. Before setting up his own Wi-Fi connection, he realized that his neighbors have an open Wi-Fi network.

Can Michael use his neighbors' Wi-Fi network without their knowledge?

Yes   No

CASE STUDY D

Sarah's next-door neighbor David left on a lengthy vacation. It is difficult to find parking on their street, and David's driveway—situated smack in between their two homes—is now empty. Sarah wishes to park her car there while her neighbor is away.

Should Sarah be allowed to park her car in David's vacant driveway without his advance permission?

○ Yes   ○ No

FIGURE 1.1

"Right and Good" Commandments

	MITZVAH	SOURCE
	Do not stand by when someone's life is at risk.	Leviticus 19:16
	Pick up any lost object you encounter and return it to its owner.	Deuteronomy 22:1–3
	Provide roadside assistance.	Exodus 23:5
	Don't spread gossip.	Leviticus 19:16

TEXT 5

The Spirit of the Law

Nachmanides, Deuteronomy 6:18

RABBI MOSHE
BEN NACHMAN
(NACHMANIDES, RAMBAN)
1194–1270

Scholar, philosopher,
author, and physician.
Nachmanides was born
in Spain and served as
leader of Iberian Jewry. In
1263, he was summoned
by King James of Aragon
to a public disputation
with Pablo Cristiani, a
Jewish apostate. Though
Nachmanides was
the clear victor of the
debate, he had to flee
Spain because of the
resulting persecution.
He moved to Israel
and helped reestablish
communal life in
Jerusalem. He authored
a classic commentary
on the Pentateuch
and a commentary
on the Talmud.

וּלְרַבּוֹתֵינוּ בָּזֶה מִדְרָשׁ יָפֶה, אָמְרוּ זוֹ . . . לִפְנִים מִשּׁוּרַת הַדִּין. וְהַכַּוָּנָה בָּזֶה, כִּי מִתְּחִלָּה אָמַר שֶׁתִּשְׁמוֹר חֻקּוֹתָיו וְעֵדוֹתָיו אֲשֶׁר צִוָּךְ, וְעַתָּה יֹאמַר גַּם בַּאֲשֶׁר לֹא צִוְּךָ תֵּן דַּעְתְּךָ לַעֲשׂוֹת הַטּוֹב וְהַיָּשָׁר בְּעֵינָיו, כִּי הוּא אוֹהֵב הַטּוֹב וְהַיָּשָׁר.

וְזֶה עִנְיָן גָּדוֹל, לְפִי שֶׁאִי אֶפְשָׁר לְהַזְכִּיר בַּתּוֹרָה כָּל הַנְהָגוֹת הָאָדָם עִם שְׁכֵנָיו וְרֵעָיו וְכָל מַשָּׂאוֹ וּמַתָּנוֹ וְתִקּוּנֵי הַיִּשּׁוּב וְהַמְּדִינוֹת כֻּלָּם.

אֲבָל אַחֲרֵי שֶׁהִזְכִּיר מֵהֶם הַרְבֵּה, כְּגוֹן לֹא תֵלֵךְ רָכִיל (וַיִּקְרָא יט, טז), לֹא תִקֹּם וְלֹא תִטֹּר (שָׁם, יח), וְלֹא תַעֲמֹד עַל דַּם רֵעֶךָ (שָׁם, טז), לֹא תְקַלֵּל חֵרֵשׁ (שָׁם, יד), מִפְּנֵי שֵׂיבָה תָּקוּם (שָׁם, לב), וְכַיּוֹצֵא בָהֶן, חָזַר לוֹמַר בְּדֶרֶךְ כְּלָל שֶׁיַּעֲשֶׂה הַטּוֹב וְהַיָּשָׁר בְּכָל דָּבָר עַד שֶׁיִּכָּנֵס בָּזֶה . . . לִפְנִים מִשּׁוּרַת הַדִּין.

Our sages expounded on this verse and explained that it instructs us to . . . go beyond the letter of the law. In other words, the Torah first exhorts us to observe all of G-d's commandments, and it now instructs us to be careful to do that which is "right and good," even when not explicitly commanded to do so, because G-d cherishes good and proper conduct.

This instruction is very important because it would be impossible for the Torah to exhaustively address all of our conduct with

Watch a conversation with
**Rabbi Adin Even-Israel
Steinsaltz** about Talmudic
ethics and the laws
they inspire:
myjli.com/beyondright

our friends and neighbors, all of our business affairs, and the welfare of society and the world.

Instead, after offering multiple specific commandments such as, "You shall not go about as a gossipmonger" (LEVITICUS 19:16), "Do not take revenge or bear a grudge" (IBID., 19:18), "Do not stand by the shedding of your fellow's blood" (IBID., 19:16), "Do not curse even a deaf person" (IBID., 19:14), and "Stand in the presence of the aged" (IBID., 19:32), the Torah then concludes with a generalized command to do that which is "right and good" . . . meaning, to go beyond the letter of the law.

**TRIPTYCH OF GOODNESS
CHESED—ACTS OF
LOVING KINDNESS**
Chaia Heller, Leverett, MA

TEXT 6

Sodom-Like Conduct

Talmud, Bava Batra 12b

כּוֹפִין עַל מִדַּת סְדוֹם.

A person is compelled by law not to act in a manner characteristic of the inhabitants of Sodom.

BABYLONIAN TALMUD

A literary work of monumental proportions that draws upon the legal, spiritual, intellectual, ethical, and historical traditions of Judaism. The 37 tractates of the Babylonian Talmud contain the teachings of the Jewish sages from the period after the destruction of the 2nd Temple through the 5th century CE. It has served as the primary vehicle for the transmission of the Oral Law and the education of Jews over the centuries; it is the entry point for all subsequent legal, ethical, and theological Jewish scholarship.

Detail from one of the most elaborate copies of Maimonides's classic work, the *Mishneh Torah*. Illuminated in Northern Italy, c. 1457, the manuscript is attributed to the Master of the Barbo Missal. The parchment manuscript contains several large depictions of various aspects of the law in tempera and gold leaf. This scene, an introduction to the laws pertaining to death and the ritual impurity it causes, depicts part of the care and purification given to a corpse prior to burial. This process is a Jewish value known as *chesed shel emet*—true kindness—since the recipient is unable to give anything in return. (Jointly owned by the Israel Museum, Jerusalem, and The Metropolitan Museum of Art, New York)

TEXT 7A

Mine Is Mine, Yours Is Yours

Mishnah, Avot 5:10

הָאוֹמֵר שֶׁלִּי שֶׁלִּי וְשֶׁלְּךָ שֶׁלָּךְ, זוֹ מִדָּה בֵּינוֹנִית.
וְיֵשׁ אוֹמְרִים, זוֹ מִדַּת סְדוֹם.

One who insists, "What is mine is mine, and what is yours is yours," is of average character. However, another opinion maintains that such an attitude is characteristic of the wicked people of Sodom.

AVOT
(ETHICS OF THE FATHERS; PIRKEI AVOT)

A 6-chapter work on Jewish ethics that is studied widely by Jewish communities, especially during the summer. The first 5 chapters are from the Mishnah, tractate Avot. Avot differs from the rest of the Mishnah in that it does not focus on legal subjects; it is a collection of the sages' wisdom on topics related to character development, ethics, healthy living, piety, and the study of Torah.

TEXT 7B

Character Assessment

Rabbi Menachem Me'iri, ad loc.

שְׁתֵּיהֶן אֱמֶת, וְהוּא שֶׁאִם בְּמָה שֶׁאֵינוֹ רוֹצֶה שֶׁיֵּהָנוּ אֲחֵרִים
מִמֶּנּוּ הוּא דָבָר שֶׁאִלּוּ הָיָה מְהַנֶּה אוֹתָם בְּכָךְ לֹא הָיָה אֶצְלוֹ
אוֹ אֵצֶל מָמוֹנוֹ שׁוּם חִסָּרוֹן, זוֹ הִיא מִדַּת סְדוֹם . . .

אֲבָל הָרִאשׁוֹנָה הִיא שֶׁאִלּוּ מְהַנֵּהוּ יֵשׁ אֶצְלוֹ אוֹ אֵצֶל
מָמוֹנוֹ קְצָת חִסָּרוֹן . . . וְעַכָּבָה זוֹ הוֹאִיל וְיֵשׁ בָּהּ חִסָּרוֹן
אֵינָהּ מִדַּת סְדוֹם, שֶׁאֵינוֹ רוֹצֶה לַחֲסֵר בְּשֶׁל אֲחֵרִים וְלֹא
לְהִתְחַסֵּר עַל יְדֵי אֲחֵרִים, אֶלָּא הִיא מִדָּה בֵּינוֹנִית.

Both statements in the Mishnah are valid, because the second view [which classifies such conduct as wicked] refers to those who refuse to permit others to benefit from them,

RABBI MENACHEM ME'IRI
1249–1310

Talmudist and author. Me'iri was born in Provence, France. His monumental work, *Beit Habechirah*, summarizes in a lucid style the discussions of the Talmud along with the commentaries of the major subsequent rabbis. Despite its stature, the work was largely unknown for many generations, and thus has had less influence on subsequent Halachic development.

even when they will incur no personal or monetary expense as a result. Such conduct is characteristic of the inhabitants of Sodom. . . .

By contrast, the first view in the Mishnah [which classifies such conduct as "average"] refers to those who refuse to allow others to benefit from them when doing so *would* come at a personal or monetary expense. . . . Individuals who adopt this approach cannot be compared to the inhabitants of Sodom because they seek simply to avoid incurring losses through the actions of others, just as they would not inflict a loss upon their fellow. This indeed reflects the average character.

Detail from the introductory artwork to the Book of Damages in the Master of the Barbo Missal's 15th-century illumination of Maimonides's *Mishneh Torah* depicting damage that can be caused by an animal. (Jointly owned by the Israel Museum, Jerusalem, and The Metropolitan Museum of Art, New York)

TEXT 8

Walls and Windows

Maimonides, *Mishneh Torah,* Laws of Neighbors 7:8

**RABBI MOSHE
BEN MAIMON
(MAIMONIDES, RAMBAM)
1135–1204**

Halachist, philosopher,
author, and physician.
Maimonides was born
in Córdoba, Spain. After
the conquest of Córdoba
by the Almohads, he fled
Spain and eventually
settled in Cairo, Egypt.
There, he became the
leader of the Jewish
community and served
as court physician to
the vizier of Egypt.
He is most noted for
authoring the *Mishneh
Torah,* an encyclopedic
arrangement of
Jewish law; and for his
philosophical work,
Guide for the Perplexed.
His rulings on Jewish
law are integral to
the formation of
Halachic consensus.

מִי שֶׁהָיוּ לוֹ חַלּוֹנוֹת לְמַטָּה בְּכָתְלוֹ וּבָא חֲבֵרוֹ
לִבְנוֹת בִּפְנֵיהֶן וְאָמַר לוֹ, אֲנִי אֶפְתַּח לְךָ חַלּוֹנוֹת
אֲחֵרוֹת בְּכֹתֶל זֶה עַצְמוֹ לְמַעְלָה מֵאֵלוּ . . .

אִם לֹא הָיָה שָׁם טֹרַח כְּלָל וְאֵין צָרִיךְ לְפַנּוֹת, אֵינוֹ יָכוֹל
לְעַכֵּב עָלָיו. וְכוֹפִין אוֹתוֹ שֶׁיִּהְיֶה חֲבֵרוֹ סוֹתֵם חַלּוֹן זֶה
שֶׁלְּמַטָּה מִמֶּנּוּ וְעוֹשֶׂה לוֹ חַלּוֹן מִלְמַעְלָה, שֶׁזוֹ מִדַּת סְדוֹם.

וְכֵן כָּל דָּבָר שֶׁזֶּה נֶהֱנֶה בּוֹ וְאֵין חֲבֵרוֹ מַפְסִיד
וְאֵין חָסֵר כְּלוּם, כּוֹפִין עָלָיו.

A person has windows set in the lower portion
of the wall of his house, and his neighbor
desires to erect a building that would block
them. The neighbor proposes to solve the
problem by installing new windows in the
upper portion of the homeowner's wall. . . .

If this arrangement won't cause the homeowner
any difficulty at all and would not require him
to leave his home during the construction,
he cannot prevent the new neighbor from
performing this construction. The homeowner
is compelled by law to allow the neighbor to
close the windows on the bottom part of his
wall and create new windows higher up. This is

For an introduction
to the processes of a
modern Jewish
rabbinical court, watch:
myjli.com/beyondright

because it would be Sodom-like conduct for the homeowner to refuse this accommodation.

This principle applies to every situation in which one individual will benefit while his fellow will not lose anything as a result. In all such cases, the relevant party is compelled by law to cooperate.

THERE'S MORE...

For an additional example of the implementation of the anti-Sodom-like conduct principle, see Appendix A (p. 29).

QUESTION

How might Jewish law adjudicate Case Studies A and B?

Professor Michael Helfand explains the process of religious arbitration and its place in the contemporary legal system:
myjli.com/beyondright

No Pain, Only Gain

Talmud, Bava Kama 20a–21b

הַדָּר בַּחֲצַר חֲבֵרוֹ שֶׁלֹּא מִדַּעְתּוֹ צָרִיךְ
לְהַעֲלוֹת לוֹ שָׂכָר אוֹ אֵין צָרִיךְ . . .

בְּחָצֵר דְּלֹא קַיְמָא לְאַגְרָא וְגַבְרָא דְּעָבִיד לְמֵיגַּר מַאי?

מָצֵי אָמַר לֵיה מַאי חֲסַרְתִּיךְ?

אוֹ דִּלְמָא מַצֵי אָמַר הָא אִתְהֲנֵית . . .

הַאי זֶה נֶהֱנֶה וְזֶה לֹא חָסֵר הוּא. . . .

אָמַר לֵיה רַבָּה בַּר רַב הוּנָא, הָכֵי אָמַר אַבָּא מָרִי
מִשְּׁמֵיה דְּרַב: אֵינוֹ צָרִיךְ לְהַעֲלוֹת לוֹ שָׂכָר.

If one lives in his fellow's yard without the latter's
knowledge, does he have to pay him rent or not? . . .

The question is in regard to a yard that is not
on the market for rent, but the squatter is a
person who usually rents. What is the law?

Can the squatter say to the owner,
"What loss have I caused you?"

Or, perhaps the owner can insist, "Look,
you have benefited [from my property
instead of paying rent elsewhere]!" . . .

This is a case in which one individual benefits
while the other does not lose anything. . . .

[The Talmud concludes:] Rabah the son of Rav Huna stated, "My father ruled in the name of Rav that the squatter does not have to pay rent."

TEXT 10

Right to Refuse

Tosafot, Bava Batra 12b

הָא דְּכוֹפִין עַל מִדַּת סְדוֹם בְּזֶה נֶהֱנֶה וְזֶה לֹא חָסֵר, הַיְינוּ בְּשֶׁכְּבָר דָּר בַּחֲצַר חֲבֵרוֹ, שֶׁאֵינוּ מַעֲלֶה לוֹ שָׂכָר.

אֲבָל הָא פְּשִׁיטָא שֶׁיָּכוֹל לִמְחוֹת בּוֹ שֶׁלֹּא יִכָּנֵס לָדוּר בְּבֵיתוֹ.

We only compel the property owner not to conduct himself like the inhabitants of Sodom regarding the past: the squatter, who resided on his property without paying rent, is not compelled to pay him rent for the past.

At the same time, it is clear that the property owner has the right to protest the squatter's presence and need not permit the squatter to remain on his property.

TOSAFOT

A collection of French and German Talmudic commentaries written during the 12th and 13th centuries. Among the most famous authors of *Tosafot* are Rabbi Yaakov Tam, Rabbi Shimshon ben Avraham of Sens, and Rabbi Yitzchak ("the Ri"). Printed in almost all editions of the Talmud, these commentaries are fundamental to basic Talmudic study.

TEXT 11

Compromising Control

Rabbi Shimon Shkop, *Chidushei Rabbi Shimon Shkop*,
Bava Kama 19:3

**RABBI SHIMON SHKOP
1860–1939**

Talmudic scholar. Born
in Turets (modern-day
Belarus), Rabbi Shkop
studied in the yeshiva
of Volozhin where he
was a close student of
the renowned Rabbi
Chayim Soloveitchik.
He taught at the yeshiva
in Telz before being
appointed to head the
yeshiva in Grodno. The
author of *Shaarei Yosher*
and other works of
Talmudic scholarship,
Rabbi Shkop is known
for his distinctive method
of analysis, focusing
on the intellectual
and philosophical
principles by which the
law is established.

וְנִרְאֶה דְכַוָּנָתָם דְלְכַתְּחִילָה לֵיכָּא כְּפִיָה מִשּׁוּם דְאִם
יִכְפּוּהוּ נוֹטְלִים מִמֶּנּוּ שְׁלִיטַת בֵּיתוֹ, וְעַל זֶה קַפְּדֵי רוֹב
אִינְשֵׁי, וְלֹא חָשִׁיב סְדוֹם בְּדָבָר שֶׁקַפְּדֵי רוֹב אִינְשֵׁי.

וְאִם כְּבָר דָּר בּוֹ, הֲרֵי כָּפוּהוּ בְּאוֹפֶן שֶׁלֹּא יִהְיֶה
נֶעֱדַר שְׁלִיטָתוֹ, דְּכָל זְמַן שֶׁיִּרְצֶה יֵצֵא מִבֵּיתוֹ.

In my opinion, the reason *Tosafot* rules that the
property owner cannot be actively compelled
to allow a squatter on his property is because
compulsion in such an instance would be a forcible
negation of the property owner's control over
his own property. Most people would object to
this. The failure of an individual to consent to
something that most people would object to
cannot be considered Sodom-like conduct.

However, the squatter's presence on the property
without the owner's knowledge doesn't negate the
owner's control of the property because the owner
retains the right to evict the squatter at any time.

QUESTION

How might Jewish law adjudicate Case Studies C and D?

THERE'S MORE...

For an additional example of a law based on the principle of "doing what is right and good," see Appendix B (p. 31).

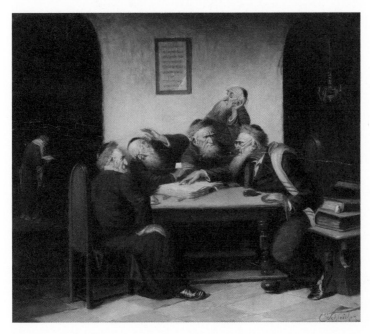

EINE STREITFRAGE AUS DEM TALMUD—A CONTROVERSY IN THE TALMUD
Carl Schleicher, oil on panel, 19th century, Germany

III. RECOMMENDED CONDUCT

While Jewish law will not compel an individual to suffer a loss in order to allow benefit to a second party, it does delineate guidelines for circumstances under which such conduct is expected on an ethical basis. The following case from the Talmud illustrates this moral expectation.

TEXT 12

Ways of the Righteous

Talmud, Bava Metzi'a 83a

רַבָּה בַּר בַּר חָנָן תְּבָרוּ לֵיה הַנְהוּ שַׁקוֹלָאֵי חָבִיתָא דְחַמְרָא, שָׁקַל לִגְלִימַיְיהוּ.

אָתוּ אָמְרוּ לְרַב, אָמַר לֵיה, הַב לְהוּ גְלִימַיְיהוּ.

אָמַר לֵיה, דִּינָא הָכֵי?

אָמַר לֵיה אִין, לְמַעַן תֵּלֵךְ בְּדֶרֶךְ טוֹבִים (מִשְׁלֵי ב, כ).

יָהֵיב לְהוּ גְלִימַיְיהוּ.

אָמְרוּ לֵיה, עֲנִיֵּי אֲנַן וְטָרְחִינַן כּוּלֵּה יוֹמָא וּכְפִינַן וְלֵית לָן מִידֵי.

אָמַר לֵיה, זִיל הַב אַגְרַיְיהוּ.

אָמַר לֵיה, דִּינָא הָכֵי?

אָמַר לֵיה אִין, וְאָרְחוֹת צַדִּיקִים תִּשְׁמוֹר (מִשְׁלֵי ב, כ).

Rabah bar bar Chanan's barrel of wine was
negligently broken by the porters he hired
to transport it. Rabah seized the porters'
cloaks as payment for the damage.

The porters complained to Rav, who instructed Rabah, "Give them back their cloaks."

Rabah asked, "Is that the law?"

Rav replied, "Yes—as stated in the verse, 'In order that you follow the path of the good people.'" (PROVERBS 2:20)

Rabah returned the porters their cloaks.

The porters complained further to Rav, "We are poor and we labored all day. Now we are hungry and have nothing to eat."

Rav told Rabah, "Pay them their wages."

Rabah asked, "Is that the law?"

Rav responded, "Yes—as stated in the verse, 'And observe the ways of the righteous'" (PROVERBS 2:20).

THERE'S MORE...

For a more detailed analysis of this Talmudic episode and its implications, see the Case Analysis on page 34.

FIGURE 1.2

The Three Degrees of "Doing What Is Right and Good" in Jewish Law

A.   Obligations specified by the Torah's explicit commandments, such as those detailed in Figure 1.1. These laws are obligatory for everyone.

B.   Doing the right thing in favor of a fellow when no personal expense is incurred. Such conduct was made legally binding by rabbinic law.

C.   Doing the right thing in favor of a fellow despite personal expense or loss. Such conduct is not legally obligatory, but is nevertheless encouraged.

Cover artwork to the six chapters of *Ethics of the Fathers* included in a late 15th-century manuscript of a Sefardic prayer book. (Library of the JTS, New York [MS 8235])

EXERCISE 1.2

We identified three degrees of expression of the basic Jewish principle of doing what is "right and good." Identify the areas in your life in which you might better apply each of these degrees.

a

b

c

d

ELIEZER AND REBECCA AT THE WELL
Illustration from *Dore's English Bible*, 1866. In this story from Genesis, Eliezer experiences Rebecca's great kindness to himself and his animals after a long journey.

KEY POINTS

1   All legal systems are shaped by their underlying values, but this is especially true of Jewish law.

2   While secular law views its purpose as maintaining social order by protecting individual rights, Jewish law sees its purpose as shaping society by guiding individuals to do what is right and upstanding in G-d's eyes.

3   Jewish law forbids spiteful conduct. "Spite fences" are forbidden, and people can be compelled to allow changes to their property that benefit others and come at no personal cost.

4   Certain unauthorized uses of other people's property that cause no harm to the owners are permitted by Jewish law. However, the owner generally retains the right to object.

5   When doing the right thing in favor of a fellow entails a degree of personal expense or loss, Jewish law declines to mandate it, but nevertheless encourages people to adopt this praiseworthy approach.

APPENDIX A

TEXT 13

Mill Rental

Talmud, Ketubot 103a

הַהוּא גַּבְרָא דְּאוֹגַר לֵיהּ רֵיחַיָּא לְחַבְרֵיהּ
לִטְחִינָה. לְסוֹף אִיעַתַּר זַבִּין רֵיחַיָּא וְחַמָּר.

אָמַר לֵיהּ, עַד הָאִידְנָא הֲוָה טְחִינְנָא
גַּבָּךְ, הַשְׁתָּא הַב לִי אַגְרָא.

אָמַר לֵיהּ, מִיטְחַן טְחִינְנָא לָךְ . . .

וְלֹא אֲמָרָן אֶלָּא דְּלֵית לֵיהּ טְחִינָא לְרֵיחַיָּא.

אֲבָל אִית לֵיהּ טְחִינָא לְרֵיחַיָּא כְּגוֹן זוֹ,
כּוֹפִין אוֹתוֹ עַל מִדַּת סְדוֹם.

A man once rented his mill to his fellow in exchange for milling services [whereby the renter would pay for the rental by grinding the owner's grain upon demand]. Later, the mill owner became rich. He purchased another mill and a donkey, and no longer required the renter's grinding services.

The mill owner said to the renter, "Until now you milled my grain as rent payment for the mill. Now, since I no longer require this service, give me cash payments for the millstone."

The renter replied, "I will grind for you because that is what I agreed to. I never agreed to pay cash." . . .

The renter's response is justified if there isn't enough local demand for grinding services to operate the mill full-time, and he would use the slack time to grind the owner's grain and thereby pay his rent. Under such circumstances, switching to cash payment would cause the renter an actual loss.

However, if there is sufficient local demand for grinding services to operate the mill full-time, and instead of grinding the owner's grain the renter can grind for other people for a fee, thereby earning the money needed to pay for the rental, he is compelled by law not to act like the inhabitants of Sodom and pay his rental fee in cash.

SODOM AND GOMORAH
Natalia Kadish, colored pencil
on dark mat board, 2011

APPENDIX B

TEXT 14

Neighbor's Rights

Maimonides, *Mishneh Torah*, Laws of Neighbors 12:5

הַמּוֹכֵר קַרְקַע שֶׁלּוֹ לְאַחֵר, יֵשׁ לַחֲבֵרוֹ שֶׁהוּא בְּצַד
הַמֵּצֶר שֶׁלּוֹ לִתֵּן דָּמִים לַלּוֹקֵחַ וּלְסַלֵּק אוֹתוֹ.

וְדָבָר זֶה מִשּׁוּם שֶׁנֶּאֱמַר וְעָשִׂיתָ הַיָּשָׁר וְהַטּוֹב (דְּבָרִים ו, יח).
אָמְרוּ חֲכָמִים, הוֹאִיל וְהַמֶּכֶר אֶחָד הוּא טוֹב וְיָשָׁר
הוּא שֶׁיִּקְנֶה מָקוֹם זֶה בֶּן הַמֵּצֶר יוֹתֵר מִן הָרָחוֹק.

If someone sells property to someone other than
the neighbor who owns the adjacent property,
the neighbor has the right to reimburse the
buyer for the purchase and evict him. . . .

This law is based on the verse, "Do what is
right and good" (DEUTERONOMY 6:18).
The sages explained that since the sale price
is the same, it is "right and good" that the
property should be acquired by a neighbor
rather than by a distant person.

Perspectives on the Functions of Law

July 4, 1776

We hold these truths to be self-evident, that all men are created equal, that they are endowed by their Creator with certain unalienable Rights, that among these are Life, Liberty and the pursuit of Happiness.

That to secure these rights, Governments are instituted among Men, deriving their just powers from the consent of the governed . . .

| England, 1690

Second Treatise of Civil Government, Chapter XI, "Of the Extent of the Legislative Power"

The end of law is not to abolish or restrain, but to preserve and enlarge freedom: for in all the states of created beings capable of laws, where there is no law, there is no freedom: for liberty is, to be free from restraint and violence from others; which cannot be, where there is no law: but freedom is not, as we are told, a liberty for every man to do what he lists: (for who could be free, when every other man's humour might domineer over him?) but a liberty to dispose and order as he lists, his person, actions, possessions, and his whole property, within the allowance of those laws under which he is, and therein not to be subject to the arbitrary will of another, but freely follow his own.

| England, 1651

The Leviathan, Chapter XIII

Hereby it is manifest that during the time men live without a common power to keep them all in awe, they are in that condition which is called war; and such a war as is a war of every man against every man. . . .

Where every man is enemy to every man, the same results occur in the time when men live without other security than what their own strength and their own invention shall furnish them with. In such condition there is no place for industry, because the fruit thereof is uncertain: and consequently no culture of the earth; no navigation, nor use of the commodities that may be imported by sea; no commodious [large or spacious] building; no instruments of moving and removing such things as require much force; no knowledge of the face of the earth; no account of time; no arts; no letters; no society; and which is worst of all, continual fear, and danger of violent death; and the life of man, solitary, poor, nasty, brutish, and short. . . .

It may be perceived what manner of life there would be, where there is no common power to fear, by the manner of life which men that have formerly lived under a peaceful government use to degenerate into a civil war.

RABBI YITZCHAK ARAMEH

📖 *Akeidat Yitzchak, Shaar 46*

Spain, second half of fifteenth century

The divine interpersonal laws are unique. Only G-d, the all-knowing Creator of the world, can perceive the real nature of people and their possessions and establish a true system of justice, as the verse says, "He Who forms the hearts of all, Who understands everything they do" (Psalms 33:15).

The prophet says, "You are great in counsel and mighty in carrying it out, for Your eyes are open to the ways of all people, to give each person in accordance with their ways and in accordance with the fruit of their deeds" (Jeremiah 32:19). Only G-d, who is "great in counsel and mighty in carrying it out," and who created the world and all that it contains with this power, can establish a system that properly "gives each person in accordance with their ways" and judges them according to their true nature. . . .

The Torah's interpersonal laws naturally generate the benefit of guiding people's impulses and correcting their character. This is in addition to establishing and maintaining a more sound societal order than can be produced by any human system of law.

RABBI NATAN LEVIN

📖 *Beit Yitzchak, Choshen Mishpat, Bepetach Habayit*

Poland, 1906

The interpersonal laws commanded by the Torah are filled with the spirit of holiness because they were established and commanded by G-d. Secular legal systems attend to regulating society. The Jewish system does likewise in an exceptionally advanced manner, but it also possesses a refined spirit of holiness that uplifts and purifies those who observe it. . . .

For this reason, the Torah's interpersonal laws begin with the commandment to honor one's parents, establishing the proper relationship between parents and their children. This commandment serves as a foundation for all the subsequent laws concerning societal order; it is a cornerstone of this great edifice. . . .

Secular legal systems aim to resolve conflict. They regulate conduct in work and business transactions based on principles of justice, with the purpose of removing wrongdoing and offense.

The Torah laws similarly resolve disputes and straighten crooked paths, but they simultaneously plant seeds of peace to draw people together and uproot the causes of conflicts and quarrels. Therefore, Jewish courts are commanded to pursue settlements of compromise between disputants. These efforts are commanded by the verse, "Render true and peaceful judgment in your courts (Zechariah 8:16)"—for, as our sages explain, "peaceful judgment" refers to compromise settlements (Sanhedrin 6b).

Case Analysis

The case from the Talmud cited in Text 12 appears here with explanation and analysis culled from the classic Talmudic commentaries and Halachic works.

① The Talmud presents a case in which a wine barrel was broken as a result of the porters' negligence. An example of such negligence would be if they exercised insufficient caution that led to them stumbling despite walking on level ground. Or, alternatively, if they employed an unsuitable method of carrying the barrel.

Rashi, ad loc.

Since the accident occurred as result of the porters' negligence, they were legally obligated to pay compensation for the damages and were not entitled to payment for the job they botched. But had the porters not been negligent, they would not have been liable to pay for the damages.

Maharsha, ad loc.

---

② Jewish law permits individuals to exercise self-help for the sake of recovering their money or property. However, although this passage seemingly justifies a creditor seizing any property belonging to the debtor in order to recover his overdue debt, the accepted law restricts creditors to the seizure of actual items that are owed to them, but nothing else.

Shulchan Aruch Harav, Choshen Mishpat, Laws of Stolen Property **27–28**

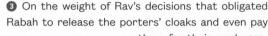

Talmud, Bava Metzi'a 83a

Rabah the grandson of Chanan once hired porters to transport his barrel of wine, but they broke it in transit. **①** He seized the porters' cloaks as payment for the damage. **②**

The porters complained to Rav, who instructed Rabah, "Give them back their cloaks."

Rabah asked, "But is that the law?"

Rav replied, "Yes **③** —as stated in the verse, 'in order that you follow the path of the good people' (Proverbs 2:20)." **④**

Rabah returned the cloaks to the porters.

The porters complained further to Rav, "We are poor and we labored all day. Now we are hungry and have nothing to eat."

Rav told Rabah, "Pay them their wages."

Rabah asked, "But is that the law?"

Rav responded, "Yes—as stated in the verse, 'and observe the ways of the righteous' (Proverbs 2:20)." **⑤**

---

③ On the weight of Rav's decisions that obligated Rabah to release the porters' cloaks and even pay them for their work, certain Halachic authorities conclude that a Jewish court has a similar capacity to compel individuals to step beyond the strict letter of the law when the court deems such action appropriate. An example of this would be in the case of a wealthy individual for whom the expense could be accurately considered relatively minimal.

Mordechai, **Bava Metzi'a 2:257**

However, other Halachic authorities reject the premise that a Jewish court can legally compel an individual to act beyond the letter of the law. Their reading of the Talmud's case is that an individual may be instructed and strongly encouraged to act beyond the letter of the law—but not legally compelled to do so. This opinion is accepted as definitive.

Shulchan Aruch,
Choshen Mishpat **12:2**

---

④ Rav employed a quote from Proverbs to justify his directives to Rabah. However, elsewhere the Talmud derives the virtue of acting beyond the strict letter of the law from an alternative verse: "Inform them about the way they should follow and the deeds they should do" (Exodus 18:20). The Talmud explains that the words "they should do" refer to going beyond the letter of the law (Bava Metzi'a 30b).

Tosafot observes that an examination of various Talmudic discussions on the topic reveals the deliberate use of a varied pool of scriptural sources to establish the value of stepping beyond the letter of the law. Tosafot views these nuances as indicative of a hierarchy within the virtue of acting beyond the letter of the law. The hierarchy starts with a category close to the baseline law and progresses with categories that move gradually further beyond the letter of the law. As a rule, the closer a given act is to the actual law, the greater the moral imperative to adopt its practice.

The most elementary degree of acting beyond the letter of the law occurs when an individual has a specific personal exemption from a general principle of law. In such a case, the virtue of acting beyond the letter of the law calls on the exempted individual not to make use of the dispensation. An example: Respected elderly individuals are not obligated by Jewish law to proactively trouble themselves to retrieve a lost item for the sake of returning it to its owner. In such a

case, the virtue of acting beyond the letter of the law encourages the respected elder to nevertheless act in accordance with the legal standard required of the average person.

Progressing further, a second category includes actions from which all people are equally exempt, but that would not result in the individual incurring any actual financial loss. For example: a situation in which an individual encounters a lost object and the particular circumstances are such that Jewish law frees all individuals equally from having to return the item to its owner. Considering that returning the item does not entail any financial loss, acting beyond the letter of the law would involve returning the item despite the absence of a legal obligation.

A third degree of acting beyond the letter of the law includes cases in which the action results in financial loss. Our Talmudic case study is a prime example of this category. From a strictly legal perspective, Rabah was entitled to seize compensation from the porters for the financial loss they inflicted on him. He was certainly not obligated to extend money to pay the porters for their botched job. Nevertheless, Rabah was urged to go far beyond the letter of the law and incur the financial

expenses of relinquishing his compensation and providing the withheld payments.

Tosafot, Bava Metzi'a 24b

⑤ Rabbi Eliyahu of Vilna notes that Rav used two different phrases from the same verse in response to the two questions raised by the case. In response to the question of forgiving compensation for the damage caused by the negligent porters, Rav cited the words "follow the path of the good people." By contrast, in response to the question of paying the workers for the botched job, he cited the phrase, "observe the ways of the righteous" (from the continuation of the same verse).

Adding to the categories of "beyond the letter of the law" conduct developed by *Tosafot*, Rabbi Eliyahu explains that Rav presented another two distinct levels of exemplary conduct. Forgiving compensation one is legally entitled to receive, Rabbi Eliyahu explains, is the "good" course of action, whereas going even further and extending money not owed in the first place (i.e., paying the porters for their failed job) is the "righteous" course of action.

Rabbi Eliyahu of Vilna, Proverbs 2:20

LESSON

2

ELUL
Karin Foreman, Digital Mixed Media, 2018. The Jewish month of Elul precedes the High Holidays and is a time for reflection and repentance.

BEYOND RESTITUTION

Offender rehabilitation is a value all can agree on, but does it have a role to play in the legal system? This lesson explores the Jewish value of rehabilitation, known as teshuvah: *who can do it, how it is done, what it achieves, and the roles we and our legal systems can play in facilitating it.*

I. THE LAW OF RETURN

Today's study leads us into a uniquely Jewish perspective on repentance, repair, and personal response to sin, misstep, and error—which in Judaism's view are all branches of a more powerful experience referred to as *teshuvah*. In particular, we will explore the manner in which this phenomenon is expressed in Jewish law.

First, a couple of clarifications are in order. The concept of *teshuvah* is often misunderstood, and it requires an accurate definition. It is also necessary to clarify who can experience *teshuvah*, and how they are to go about it.

TEXT 1

An Antisemite Discovers That He Is Jewish

Andrew Russel, "Former Anti-Semitic Hungarian Politician Csanad Szegedi Forced to Leave Canada," globalnews.ca, December 2013

A speaking engagement by former antisemitic Hungarian politician Csanad Szegedi, scheduled to be held in Montreal tonight, was cancelled after Szegedi was forced to leave Canada.

Szegedi is a former leader of the Hungarian nationalist Jobbik party—known for its extreme far-right and antisemitic views—until he [embraced] Judaism after discovering his Jewish heritage.

The Chabad of Westmount Educational Centre in Montreal had invited Szegedi to tell his story entitled "My Journey from Hater to Fighter of Hatred," but a video presentation was played instead after Canadian immigration officials forced Szegedi to leave the country. There were rumblings that Szegedi was asked to leave Canada after complaints were made from within the Jewish community.

Roughly 200 people attended the presentation, which became heated at times with people standing and yelling.

"I acknowledge that I have a lot of sins. And this is why I understand those people who are not happy with me being here. But these sins I try to rectify not only at the verbal level but at the level of my actions," said Szegedi in his taped message. "I have to tell the Canadian Jewish community . . . that I am exactly such a Jew as they are. I cannot help it—as you cannot help it."

ON THE EVE OF YOM KIPPUR
Jakub Weinles (1870–1938), oil on canvas, Poland (National Museum, Warsaw)

EXERCISE 2.1

Would you ever be open to accepting Csanad Szegedi as a member of the Jewish community in good standing?

◯ Yes ◯ No

If yes, what would he have to do in order to earn acceptance from you?

What might be the key elements of genuine repentance?

1.

2.

3.

4.

5.

The Cervera Bible, completed in 14th-century Cervera (present day Catalonia, Spain) is a rare manuscript that survived the destruction of the Jewish communities of Castile and Aragon in the 14th and 15th centuries. The different portions of the text were copied by scribes Yehoshua ben Avraham ibn Gaon and Shmuel ben Avraham ibn Natan, and illuminated by artist Yosef Asarfati. In this detail, Jonah is cast off of the ship as he tries to run away from G-d after receiving instructions to encourage the wicked people of Ninveh to repent. (Library of Congress [2021668000])

TEXT 2

Teshuvah for All

Maimonides, *Mishneh Torah*, Laws of *Teshuvah* 1:3

הַתְּשׁוּבָה מְכַפֶּרֶת עַל כָּל הָעֲבֵרוֹת. אֲפִלּוּ רָשָׁע
כָּל יָמָיו וְעָשָׂה תְּשׁוּבָה בָּאַחֲרוֹנָה, אֵין מַזְכִּירִין לוֹ
שׁוּם רִשְׁעוֹ. שֶׁנֶּאֱמַר, "וְרִשְׁעַת הָרָשָׁע לֹא יִכָּשֶׁל
בָּהּ בְּיוֹם שׁוּבוֹ מֵרִשְׁעוֹ" (יְחֶזְקֵאל לג, יב).

Teshuvah atones for all sins. Even if one was
wicked their entire life and did *teshuvah* at the last
moment—their wickedness is no longer held against
them. This is the meaning of the verse "a wicked
person will not stumble due to their wickedness on
the day they do *teshuvah* for it" (EZEKIEL 33:12).

RABBI MOSHE BEN MAIMON (MAIMONIDES, RAMBAM) 1135-1204

Halachist, philosopher, author, and physician. Maimonides was born in Córdoba, Spain. After the conquest of Córdoba by the Almohads, he fled Spain and eventually settled in Cairo, Egypt. There, he became the leader of the Jewish community and served as court physician to the vizier of Egypt. He is most noted for authoring the *Mishneh Torah*, an encyclopedic arrangement of Jewish law; and for his philosophical work, *Guide for the Perplexed*. His rulings on Jewish law are integral to the formation of Halachic consensus.

The title and opening paragraph of Maimonides's *Mishneh Torah*, Laws of *Teshuvah* in a manuscript dated to c. 1200 copied by Yafet ben Solomon. This handwritten manuscript contains several poems written in Maimonides's honor, as well as the signature of Maimonides himself, approving that this manuscript was copied from his personal manuscript. (Bodleian Library, Oxford, U.K., [MS. Hunt. 80])

FIGURE 2.1

The Scope of *Teshuvah*

Everything—"*Teshuvah* atones for all sins"

Everyone—"Even if one was wicked their entire life"

Anytime—"Even . . . at the last moment"

FIGURE 2.2

Five Steps of *Teshuvah*

For the source texts for these five steps, see Appendix (p. 61)

5. Verbal confession to G-d and statement of remorse and resolution for the future

4. Appeasement of the victim

3. Restitution for financial damages

2. Remorse for the offense

1. Resolution not to reoffend

Learn more about
forgiveness in
Jewish thought:
myjli.com/beyondright

II. BETTER THAN BEFORE

Judaism's concept of *teshuvah* involves more than atoning for past misdeeds. *Teshuvah* serves as an engine for personal growth that carries individuals to new heights, thereby realizing the ultimate purpose of their creation. Accordingly, G-d not only enables *teshuvah* but He actively facilitates it.

TEXT 3

Returnee Superiority

Talmud, Berachot 34b

מָקוֹם שֶׁבַּעֲלֵי תְּשׁוּבָה עוֹמְדִין צַדִּיקִים גְּמוּרִים אֵינָם עוֹמְדִין.

In the place where returnees stand, even completely righteous people cannot stand.

BABYLONIAN TALMUD

A literary work of monumental proportions that draws upon the legal, spiritual, intellectual, ethical, and historical traditions of Judaism. The 37 tractates of the Babylonian Talmud contain the teachings of the Jewish sages from the period after the destruction of the 2nd Temple through the 5th century CE. It has served as the primary vehicle for the transmission of the Oral Law and the education of Jews over the centuries; it is the entry point for all subsequent legal, ethical, and theological Jewish scholarship.

JEWS PRAYING IN THE SYNAGOGUE ON YOM KIPPUR
Maurycy Gottleib (1856–1879), oil on canvas, Poland 1878. This impressive painting depicts the interior of a no longer extant synagogue in the artist's hometown of Drohobycz, and the artist himself is portrayed several times: as the young man in colorful striped clothing, as the young boy on the lefthand side, and perhaps reading from an open volume on the far right.

TEXT 4

Return of the Soul

Rabbi Shneur Zalman of Liadi, *Likutei Torah*, Bamidbar 73a

RABBI SHNEUR
ZALMAN OF LIADI
(ALTER REBBE)
1745–1812

Chasidic rebbe, Halachic
authority, and founder of
the Chabad movement.
The Alter Rebbe was
born in Liozna, Belarus,
and was among the
principal students of the
Magid of Mezeritch. His
numerous works include
the *Tanya*, an early
classic containing the
fundamentals of Chabad
Chasidism; and *Shulchan
Aruch HaRav*, an
expanded and reworked
code of Jewish law.

לָמָה יָרְדָה הַנְּשָׁמָה לָעוֹלָם הַזֶּה בִּכְדֵי שֶׁתְּקַבֵּל שָׂכָר אַחַר כָּךְ
בְּגַן עֵדֶן, וַהֲלֹא קֹדֶם יְרִידָתָהּ הָיְתָה בְּוַדַּאי בְּגַן עֵדֶן וְהָיְתָה
נֶהֱנֶה מִזִּיו הַשְּׁכִינָה, וּמַהוּ הַיִּתְרוֹן עַל יְדֵי יְרִידָתָהּ כו'. . .

הַתֵּרוּץ הָאֲמִתִּי הוּא כְּמַאֲמַר רז"ל, יָפָה שָׁעָה אַחַת
בִּתְשׁוּבָה וּמַעֲשִׂים טוֹבִים בָּעוֹלָם הַזֶּה מִכָּל חַיֵּי
הָעוֹלָם הַבָּא. וּכְמַאֲמַר רז"ל, בְּמָקוֹם שֶׁבַּעֲלֵי תְשׁוּבָה
עוֹמְדִין צַדִּיקִים גְּמוּרִים אֵינָם יְכוֹלִים לַעֲמֹד.

וְהִנֵּה, הַנְּשָׁמוֹת קֹדֶם יְרִידָתָן לְגוּף הֵם בְּוַדַּאי צַדִּיקִים
גְּמוּרִים. אַךְ זֶהוּ הַיִּתְרוֹן שֶׁלָּהֶם בִּירִידָתָן בְּגוּף, שֶׁנַּעֲשִׂים
בְּחִינַת בַּעֲלֵי תְשׁוּבָה שֶׁאָז הֵם לְמַעְלָה מַעְלָה מִצַּדִּיקִים.

Why did our soul descend into this physical
world if the ultimate goal is its return to Heaven,
where it enjoys the radiance of G-d's presence?
Prior to the soul's descent it was also in Heaven
and enjoyed the radiance of G-d's presence! . . .

The true answer to this question lies in the sages'
teaching, "A single moment of repentance and
good deeds in this world is greater than all of
the World to Come." Similarly, our sages taught
that "In the place where returnees stand, even
completely righteous people cannot stand."

Watch an overview of
Rabbi Shneur Zalman of
Liadi's guide to *teshuvah*:
myjli.com/beyondright

Before the soul's descent into a body, it was undoubtedly perfectly righteous. But as a result of its descent, it can experience *teshuvah* and rise to a height that is superior to that of the righteous.

TEXT 5

Extend a Hand

Yom Kippur *Machzor*, *Ne'ilah* Service

אַתָּה נוֹתֵן יָד לַפּוֹשְׁעִים, וִימִינְךָ פְּשׁוּטָה לְקַבֵּל שָׁבִים.

You extend a hand to transgressors. Your right hand stretches forth to receive penitents.

MACHZOR

Prayer book. A *machzor* is a dedicated prayer book containing the special prayers for Jewish holidays, such as Rosh Hashanah and Yom Kippur.

Watch a text-based lecture about repentance through the lens of Jewish mysticism: **myjli.com/beyondright**

The above quote is shown in a 15th-century Hebrew prayer book including the daily prayers, as well as special portions for Shabbat, holidays, and fast days. (British Library, London [MS 18230])

III. PENITENT ASSISTANCE

Emulating G-d, Jewish law introduces leniencies to encourage thieves to do *teshuvah*.

EXERCISE 2.2

What can the legal system do to encourage and assist offenders to rehabilitate themselves?

1.

2.

3.

THE WICKED SON FROM THE PASSOVER *HAGGADAH* (detail)
The Ashkenazi *Haggadah*, containing the commentary of Eleazar of Worms, was copied in 15th-century Germany by Meir Jaffe. The colorful miniatures, initial word panels, and marginal decorations were created by artist Yoel ben Shimon Feibush. (British Library, London [MS 14762])

CASE STUDY

Mark was a career criminal with a lengthy history of robberies.

One of his many victims was Jack, the owner of a New York construction company. Mark successfully stole a range of construction materials from Jack's business.

Among the stolen items, there was an expensive central air-conditioning system and a kitchen cabinet set. After lifting them from Jack's property, Mark assembled and installed them in his own home.

After decades of crime, Mark's dormant conscience began to flicker to life. Eventually he resolved to turn over a new leaf, abandon his life of crime, and pursue an honest job.

Mark came clean about his thefts and set about making restitution for them.

He tracked down Jack, who had by then retired to his new home in Los Angeles. Explaining the circumstances, Mark wished to provide reimbursement, but Jack insisted that the actual stolen items be returned to him—asserting that it was "his right" to receive their physical return and to not make do with monetary substitutes. Jack's demand raises a series of questions.

1.   The air-conditioning system was intact, but its removal from Mark's house would require him to rip out walls and ceilings, causing him significant expense. Should Mark be allowed to keep it and instead reimburse Jack for its value?

    ○ Yes   ○ No

2. Mark invested time and effort in assembling the kitchen cabinets in his home. As a result, the assembled cabinet set was evaluated to be of greater value than that of the unassembled raw materials he stole. Can Mark simply pay the value of the original unassembled set?

    ○ Yes   ○ No

3. If Mark is indeed required to return the set, should he be entitled to some compensation for the increased value of the assembled cabinets?

    ○ Yes   ○ No

4. Additionally, returning the actual stolen goods would entail significant transportation costs. Whose responsibility is it to pay the transportation bill?

    ○ Mark   ○ Jack

5. Should the fact that Mark unilaterally stepped forward and confessed his misdeed affect his responsibility to make restitution in any way?

    ○ Yes   ○ No

TEXT 6

Returning Stolen Objects

Maimonides, *Mishneh Torah*, Laws of Stolen and Lost Property 1:5

כָּל הַגּוֹזֵל חַיָּב לְהַחְזִיר הַגְּזֵלָה עַצְמָהּ, שֶׁנֶּאֱמַר
וְהֵשִׁיב אֶת הַגְּזֵלָה אֲשֶׁר גָּזָל (וַיִּקְרָא ה, כג).
וְאִם אָבְדָה אוֹ נִשְׁתַּנֵּית מְשַׁלֵּם דָּמֶיהָ . . .

אֲפִלּוּ גָּזַל קוֹרָה וּבְנָאָהּ בַּבִּירָה, הוֹאִיל וְלֹא נִשְׁתַּנֵּית דִּין
תּוֹרָה הוּא שֶׁיַּהֲרֹס אֶת כָּל הַבִּנְיָן וְיַחְזִיר קוֹרָה לִבְעָלֶיהָ.

A thief is obligated to return the exact object
that he stole, as the verse states, "They must
return the object that they have stolen"
(LEVITICUS 5:23). If the stolen object was lost
or altered, the thief must pay its value. . . .

Even if a person stole a beam and used it in the
construction of a home, Scriptural law would
require that the thief tear down the entire
building to return the beam to its owner because
the beam itself is extant and unchanged.

Detail from the introductory artwork to the Book of Damages in the Master of the Barbo Missal's 15th century illumination of Maimonides's *Mishneh Torah* depicting a man stealing from a neighbor's home. (Jointly owned by the Israel Museum, Jerusalem, and The Metropolitan Museum of Art, New York)

The Penitents' Enactment

Mishnah, Gitin 5:5

הֵעִיד רַבִּי יוֹחָנָן בֶּן גֻּדְגְּדָא . . . עַל הַמֵּרִישׁ הַגָּזוּל שֶׁבְּנָאוֹ
בַּבִּירָה, שֶׁיִּטֹּל אֶת דָּמָיו מִפְּנֵי תַּקָּנַת הַשָּׁבִים.

Rabbi Yochanan ben Gudgeda testified that
there is a rabbinic enactment . . . regarding
the case of a thief that built a stolen beam
into a building: The victim of the theft is only
entitled to monetary compensation. This
was enacted for the benefit of penitents.

MISHNAH

The first authoritative
work of Jewish law that
was codified in writing.
The Mishnah contains
the oral traditions that
were passed down from
teacher to student; it
supplements, clarifies,
and systematizes the
commandments of
the Torah. Due to the
continual persecution
of the Jewish people,
it became increasingly
difficult to guarantee
that these traditions
would not be forgotten.
Rabbi Yehudah Hanasi
therefore redacted the
Mishnah at the end
of the 2nd century. It
serves as the foundation
for the Talmud.

DECALOGUE
Yekusiel Sofer, parchment,
1768. The Ten Commandments
contain the prohibition
against stealing. Bolded
letters in the lower inscription
reveal the year in which this
parchment was created.

TEXT 8

Encouraging *Teshuvah*

Rashi, Gitin 55a

שֶׁאִם אַתָּה מַצְרִיכוֹ לְקַעֲקֵעַ בִּירָתוֹ וּלְהַחֲזִיר
מָרִישׁ עַצְמוֹ, יִמָּנַע מִלַּעֲשׂוֹת תְּשׁוּבָה.

If we require thieves to destroy their buildings
for the sake of returning the actual stolen beam,
they will be discouraged from doing *teshuvah*.

TEXT 9

Added Value

Talmud, Bava Kama 95b

שֶׁבַח שֶׁעַל גַּבֵּי גְזֵלָה, דְּגַזְלָן.

Enhancement of the actual body of the
stolen item belongs to the thief.

**RABBI
SHLOMO YITZCHAKI
(RASHI)
1040-1105**

Most noted biblical and
Talmudic commentator.
Born in Troyes, France,
Rashi studied in the
famed *yeshivot* of
Mainz and Worms. His
commentaries on the
Pentateuch and the
Talmud, which focus
on the straightforward
meaning of the text,
appear in virtually
every edition of the
Talmud and Bible.

A man does a personal reckoning
of his actions as part of the
Shema prayer before retiring at
night. Detail, border decoration
in an illuminated volume of
Maimonides's *Mishneh Torah*.
This manuscript, one of the most
elaborate copies, is believed
to have been written in Spain
or Southern France in the first
half of the 14th century, with
the artwork done in Spain and
Italy. (From the collection of
the National Library of Israel
[MS. HEB. 4*1193], Jerusalem)

TEXT 10

Reversible Changes

Rabbi Moshe Isserlis, Shulchan Aruch, *Choshen Mishpat* 362:8

RABBI MOSHE ISSERLIS (RAMA)
1525–1572

Halachist. Rama served as rabbi in Krakow, Poland, and is considered the definitive authority on Jewish law among Ashkenazic Jewry. Rama authored glosses (known as the *Mapah*) on the Shulchan Aruch, and *Darchei Moshe*, a commentary on the Halachic compendium *Arbaah Turim*.

שִׁנּוּי הַחוֹזֵר לִבְרִיָּתוֹ, כְּגוֹן עָפָר וַעֲשָׂאוֹ לְבֵנִים,
אַף עַל גַּב דְּלָא קָנָה כִּדְלְעֵיל סִימָן ש"ס, שְׁבַח
מִיהָא קָנָה, וְצָרִיךְ לְהַחֲזִיר לוֹ שִׁבְחוֹ.

If the stolen item was altered but the change is reversible—such as stolen earth fashioned into bricks—the thief cannot keep it and it must be returned. However, the added value of the item does belong to the thief, and the original owner must pay the difference.

Detail from a 13th-century compendium of liturgy and prayers for Shabbat and special days known as the Siddur Austria. The manuscript contains miniatures of the Ten Commandments. Pictured here on the right, underneath the Hebrew words "Thou shalt not steal," is a thief taking a goblet from a chest. On the left side, a judge sitting on a platform points to the thief, who has his hands behind his back. (Library of the JTS [MS 8972])

TEXT 11

Return Transport

Rabbi Yosef Caro and Rabbi Moshe Isserlis,
Shulchan Aruch, *Choshen Mishpat* 367:1

הַגּוֹזֵל אֶת חֲבֵרוֹ . . . אִם חָזַר וְהוֹדָה אֵינוֹ חַיָּב
לִרְדֹּף אַחַר הַבְּעָלִים לְהַחֲזִיר לָהֶם.

אֶלָּא יְהֵא בְּיָדוֹ עַד שֶׁיָּבוֹאוּ (וְיוֹדִיעַ אוֹתָם
(טוּר ס"א) וְיִטְלוּ אֶת שֶׁלָּהֶם).

People that stole from others . . . and confessed
the theft are not required to pursue the owners
in order to return the stolen item to them.

The confessed thief may hold onto the item, notify
the owner, and wait for them to come and collect it.

**RABBI YOSEF CARO
(MARAN, *BEIT YOSEF*)
1488-1575**

Halachic authority and
author. Rabbi Caro was
born in Spain but was
forced to flee during
the Expulsion in 1492
and eventually settled in
Safed, Israel. He authored
many works, including
the *Beit Yosef, Kesef
Mishneh*, and a mystical
work, *Magid Meisharim*.
Rabbi Caro's magnum
opus, the Shulchan Aruch
(Code of Jewish Law),
has been universally
accepted as the basis
for modern Jewish law.

Beth Hamedrash and Beth Din (House of
Learning and Judgment)—A Jewish Court,
illustration from London newspaper *The
Graphic*, August 11, 1906. The detailed drawing
depicts the members of the London Beth Din
at the time, which functioned as a Jewish
court and oversaw kosher certification.

IV. THE CAREER CRIMINAL

The examples of enactments to facilitate *teshuvah* that we have studied until now were rather limited in their scope, applying only to very specific scenarios or concerning secondary issues such as costs of return.

In this section we will study a very broad and far-reaching penitents' enactment and explore what it can teach us regarding our modern legal system.

TEXT 12

Sage Disapproval

Talmud, Bava Kama 94b

מַעֲשֶׂה בְּאָדָם אֶחָד שֶׁבִּקֵּשׁ לַעֲשׂוֹת תְּשׁוּבָה. אָמְרָה
לֵיהּ אִשְׁתּוֹ, רֵיקָה, אִם אַתָּה עוֹשֶׂה תְּשׁוּבָה אֲפִלּוּ
אַבְנֵט אֵינוֹ שֶׁלְךָ. וְנִמְנַע וְלֹא עָשָׂה תְּשׁוּבָה.

בְּאוֹתָהּ שָׁעָה אָמְרוּ, הַגַּזְלָנִין . . . שֶׁהֶחֱזִירוּ אֵין מְקַבְּלִין
מֵהֶם. וְהַמְקַבֵּל מֵהֶם אֵין רוּחַ חֲכָמִים נוֹחָה הֵימֶנּוּ.

There was an incident in which a certain person sought to perform *teshuvah*. His wife said to him, "Empty-head! If you do *teshuvah*, even the belt you are wearing is not yours!" The fellow refrained and did not do *teshuvah*.

At that time, the sages declared . . . that if thieves wish to return what they stole, their victims should not accept it from them. If the victims nevertheless do accept from the thieves, the sages are displeased with their conduct.

EXERCISE 2.3

The following text is the summary of this law and the subsequent commentary on it as presented in the Code of Jewish Law. Read the text carefully and list the caveats placed on the application of this law (some of these caveats are present in Text 12 as well).

1.

2.

3.

4.

5.

ELUL
Rebecca Schisler, acrylic on canvas, 2019, San Francisco.

Eligibility Criteria

Rabbi Yosef Caro and Rabbi Moshe Isserlis,
Shulchan Aruch, *Choshen Mishpat* 366:1

גַּזְלָן מְפוּרְסָם (שֶׁעֲסָקָיו בְּכָךְ וּתְשׁוּבָתוֹ קָשָׁה) הַבָּא
לַעֲשׂוֹת תְּשׁוּבָה מֵעַצְמוֹ, אִם אֵין הַגְּזֵלָה קַיֶּמֶת אֵין
מְקַבְּלִין מִמֶּנּוּ, כְּדֵי שֶׁלֹּא יִמָּנַע מִלַּעֲשׂוֹת תְּשׁוּבָה.

וְאִם רָצָה לָצֵאת יְדֵי שָׁמַיִם וְהֶחֱזִיר,
אֵין מוֹחִין בְּיַד הַנִּגְזָל מִלְּקַבֵּל.

When established thieves—career criminals for
whom *teshuvah* is difficult—wish to do *teshuvah*
on their own initiative, then if the stolen item is
no longer extant, their victims should not accept
compensation from them. This is to ensure that such
thieves will not be deterred from doing *teshuvah*.

However, if the thieves insist that they wish to go
beyond the letter of the law and pay compensation,
the victims are not cautioned against accepting it.

FIGURE 2.3

Caveats to the Law against Accepting
Returns from Repentant Thieves

1. **Only for a career thief.**

2. **Only if the thief came forward of his own volition.**

3. **Only if the stolen item is no longer extant.**

4. **Victims are only *advised* to not accept, but they are not required to refuse.**

5. **It is nevertheless praiseworthy for the thief to make restitution.**

TEXT 14

Tax Amnesty

Leo P. Martinez, "Federal Tax Amnesty: Crime and Punishment Revisited," *Virginia Tax Review,* vol. 10 (1991), pp. 535–583

LEO P. MARTINEZ

Professor and lawyer. A graduate of University of California, Hastings College of the Law, Leo Martinez practiced privately as a tax lawyer before joining the faculty of UC Hastings and serving as the college's dean. Martinez has lectured and written extensively on insurance and tax law.

Over the past decade, at least 29 states and the District of Columbia have conducted tax amnesties. Though the state amnesty programs varied in terms of objectives, features, and results, some generalizations can be made. The programs were generally designed by state lawmakers to achieve at least one of three objectives: 1) reap a one-time revenue windfall; 2) increase future revenues by adding the names of non-filers to state tax rolls;

and 3) improve the tax compliance rate. In order to accomplish these goals, the states usually abated both criminal and civil penalties for those who had failed to file or understated their liabilities if the taxpayer paid delinquent taxes. . . .

By revenue raised, New York's program was the most successful, generating a revenue high of $401.3 million. New Jersey's program followed, bringing in $179.7 million. Other top revenue raisers were California, Illinois, and Massachusetts, pulling in $154 million, $152.4 million, and $83.2 million, respectively. At the other end of the spectrum, more than half of the states which conducted amnesties raised less than $10 million each.

Given the broad objectives of many state amnesty programs, revenue raised is not necessarily the sole indicator of success. To many analysts and lawmakers, the long-term effects are of equal concern. Many states hoped amnesty would increase their tax base by adding more names to the tax rolls. Indeed, one study showed that states implementing tax amnesty enjoyed an annual tax revenue growth rate 0.5% higher than did non-amnesty states. Another aim of most amnesties was to raise the overall compliance rate. Preliminary studies indicate this goal was also achieved.

QUESTION

What is the motivating logic behind tax amnesty programs, and in what way is it different from the Jewish "penitents' enactments"?

EXERCISE 2.4

What can you do on a personal level to help others do *teshuvah*?

A group of Jews enters the synagogue to pray on Rosh Hashanah, on a 20th-century Jewish new year postcard captioned in Yiddish: "Come, Jews, go to the house of G-d and pray for a good year." (Musée d'Art et d'Histoire du Judaïsme, Paris [CP/1142])

KEY POINTS

1   The Jewish concept of repentance is known as
    teshuvah. *Teshuvah* can be done (a) for everything,
    (b) by everyone, and (c) at any time.

2   *Teshuvah* entails completely restoring the world to the state
    it was in before the transgression was committed. Therefore,
    in addition to regret and personal change, *teshuvah* also
    requires financial restitution and emotional appeasement.

3   Jewish values call on us to assist wrongdoers along the path of
    teshuvah. To this end, in cases of theft, Jewish law (a) allows
    substituting monetary compensation rather than return of the
    stolen item when its return would cause significant expense,
    (b) provides a thief with compensation for investments he
    made to increase the value of stolen items, and (c) places
    the cost of transporting returns on the victim of the theft.

4   When a longtime thief comes forward and wishes to do *teshuvah*,
    the Jewish legal system counsels the victims to not accept
    compensation, in order to ease the process of *teshuvah*.

5   The approach of Jewish law is motivated by Judaism's perspective
    on the value of *teshuvah*: the belief that the offender deserves the
    opportunity to do *teshuvah*, and that we all have an obligation to
    help facilitate it—even through modifications in our legal system.

APPENDIX

TEXT 15A

Personal Transformation

Maimonides, *Mishneh Torah*, Laws of *Teshuvah* 2:2

וּמַה הִיא הַתְּשׁוּבָה? הוּא שֶׁיַּעֲזֹב הַחוֹטֵא חֶטְאוֹ, וִיסִירֶנּוּ
מִמַּחֲשַׁבְתּוֹ, וְיִגְמֹר בְּלִבּוֹ שֶׁלֹּא יַעֲשֵׂהוּ עוֹד. שֶׁנֶּאֱמַר,
"יַעֲזֹב רָשָׁע דַּרְכּוֹ וְאִישׁ אָוֶן מַחְשְׁבֹתָיו" (יְשַׁעְיָה נה, ז).

וְכֵן יִתְנַחֵם עַל שֶׁעָבַר, שֶׁנֶּאֱמַר, "כִּי אַחֲרֵי
שׁוּבִי נִחַמְתִּי" (יִרְמְיָה לא, יח).

וְיָעִיד עָלָיו יוֹדֵעַ תַּעֲלוּמוֹת שֶׁלֹּא יָשׁוּב לָזֶה
הַחֵטְא לְעוֹלָם, שֶׁנֶּאֱמַר, "וְלֹא נֹאמַר עוֹד
אֱלֹקֵינוּ לְמַעֲשֵׂה יָדֵינוּ (הוֹשֵׁעַ יד, ד).

וְצָרִיךְ לְהִתְוַדּוֹת בִּשְׂפָתָיו, וְלוֹמַר עִנְיָנוֹת אֵלּוּ שֶׁגָּמַר בְּלִבּוֹ.

What constitutes *teshuvah*? *Teshuvah* is when sinners abandons their sins, removes them from their thoughts, and resolves in their heart never to commit them again. This is what the verse says, "Let the wicked forsake their ways, and the unrighteous their thoughts." (ISAIAH 55:7)

Penitents must also regret the past, as the verse states, "After I returned, I regretted." (JEREMIAH 31:18)

Penitents must reach the level where G-d, who knows the hidden, will testify about them that they will never return to this sin again, as the verse states, "We will no longer say to the work of our hands, 'you are our gods.'" (HOSEA 14:4)

They must also verbally confess their sins and state these matters that they resolved in their heart.

Making Amends

TEXT 15B

Maimonides, *Mishneh Torah*, Laws of *Teshuvah* 2:9

עֲבֵרוֹת שֶׁבֵּין אָדָם לַחֲבֵרוֹ, כְּגוֹן חוֹבֵל בַּחֲבֵרוֹ אוֹ הַמְקַלֵּל אֶת חֲבֵרוֹ אוֹ גוֹזְלוֹ וְכַיּוֹצֵא בָּהֶן, אֵינוֹ נִמְחָל לוֹ לְעוֹלָם, עַד שֶׁיִּתֵּן לַחֲבֵרוֹ מַה שֶׁהוּא חַיָּב לוֹ וִירַצֵּהוּ.

אַף עַל פִּי שֶׁהֶחֱזִיר לוֹ מָמוֹן שֶׁהוּא חַיָּב לוֹ, צָרִיךְ לְרַצּוֹתוֹ וְלִשְׁאֹל מִמֶּנּוּ שֶׁיִּמְחַל לוֹ. אֲפִלּוּ לֹא הִקְנִיט אֶת חֲבֵרוֹ אֶלָּא בִּדְבָרִים, צָרִיךְ לְפַיְּסוֹ וְלִפְגֹּעַ בּוֹ עַד שֶׁיִּמְחַל לוֹ.

Interpersonal sins, such as causing physical injury, cursing, or stealing, are never forgiven until the offender pays the necessary restitution to the victim and appeases them.

Even after repaying restitution to the victim, the offender must appease the victim and ask them for forgiveness. Even for verbally offending someone, without causing them any tangible loss, the offender must appease the victim and seek their forgiveness until it is granted.

Moses ascends a burning Mount Sinai to receive the Tablets as the Jewish people wait at the foot of the mountain below. This elaborate illustration begins the Ethics of the Fathers section in the Rothschild Mahzor, a prayer book copied in Florence, 1490. This parchment manuscript is full of detailed drawings, medallions, and marginal decorations. (Library of the JTS [MS 8892])

Books of *Teshuvah* Guidance

The concept of *teshuvah*, return to G-d and repentance from transgression, is central to Jewish thought. Over the generations, many great Jewish thinkers have devoted books, and sections within books, to the topic of *teshuvah*, explaining how it is done and the effect it has. We present here an overview of some of the major works on the topic of *teshuvah*, ranging from the twelfth century until the twentieth century.

Hilchot Teshuvah

Maimonides, Twelfth Century
First page of *Hilchot Teshuvah* from a manuscript authorized by Maimonides, currently held in the Bodleian Library (Oxford, U.K.)

As part of his comprehensive code of Jewish law entitled *Mishneh Torah*, Maimonides devoted a section to the laws of *teshuvah*. In his defense of *Mishneh Torah* against its critics, Nachmanides highlighted the section on *teshuvah* as a particularly significant work. Nachmanides explained that discussions about *teshuvah* are scattered through the Talmudic and Midrashic literature, and Maimonides was the first to develop a systematic presentation of the conclusions of these discussions.

Rabbi Moshe ben Maimon (1135–1204), also known as Rambam or Maimonides, was born in Córdoba, Spain. After the conquest of Córdoba by the Almohads, he fled Spain and eventually settled in Cairo, Egypt. There, he became the leader of the Jewish community and served as court physician to the vizier of Egypt. He is most noted for authoring the *Mishneh Torah*, an encyclopedic arrangement of Jewish law; and for his philosophical work, *Guide for the Perplexed*. His rulings on Jewish law are integral to the formation of Halachic consensus.

12TH CENTURY

Roke'ach

Rabbi Elazar of Worms, Thirteenth Century
Title page of the first edition of *Roke'ach*, published in Fano, Italy, 1505, by the famous Soncino family press

At the start of his compendium of practical Jewish law entitled *Roke'ach*, Rabbi Elazar of Worms includes a lengthy section on *teshuvah*. Rabbi Elazar formulated various methods of *teshuvah* for distinct types of transgressions and was the first to supply detailed guidance for specific *teshuvah* processes tailored to the specific kind of transgression. These teachings were subsequently edited further and published as a stand-alone work entitled *Yoreh Chata'im*. Rabbi Elazar's writings on the theme of *teshuvah* were particularly influential, and are widely quoted and expounded upon by subsequent scholars.

Rabbi Elazar ben Yehudah of Worms (c. 1160–c. 1230) was a rabbi, kabbalist, author, and liturgical poet. A student of the renowned pietist Rabbi Yehudah HaChasid, Rabbi Elazar wrote on kabbalah and the siddur, but he is best known for his Halachic work entitled *Roke'ach*. He suffered greatly from antisemitic persecution, and his wife and son were killed in a pogrom.

Shaarei Teshuvah

Rabbi Yonah of Gerona, Thirteenth Century
A fourteenth-century manuscript of *Shaarei Teshuvah*, composed in Sefardic script

Shaarei Teshuvah—*The Gates of Teshuvah*—was one section of a broader work by Rabbi Yonah of Gerona titled *Shaarei Tzedek*. Unlike the rest of the work, only this section on *teshuvah* survived. In this classic offering, Rabbi Yonah details the various steps of *teshuvah*; explores a variety of sources that provide inspiration to engage in *teshuvah*; and divides transgressions into ten categories for the sake of identifying the degree of *teshuvah* required for each category. Rabbi Yonah also authored a separate work entitled *Yesod Hateshuvah*, which supplies a concise guide for returnees.

Rabbi Yonah of Gerona (c. 1210–c. 1263) was a Spanish Talmudist and ethicist. A native of Gerona, Catalonia, Rabbi Yonah also studied with leading figures of the Tosafist school in France, thus combining Ashkenazic and Sefaradic scholarship. He wrote biblical and Talmudic commentaries and is best known for his moralistic works on repentance and ethical conduct.

Igeret Hateshuvah

Rabbi Shneur Zalman of Liadi, Eighteenth Century
Title page of the 1806 Shklov edition of *Tanya*, the first
edition to include the final version of *Igeret Hateshuvah*

Igeret Hateshuvah is a Chasidic work on *teshuvah* by
Rabbi Shneur Zalman of Liadi, published as the third
section to his foundational *Tanya*. This work emphasizes
the decision to embrace G-d and His path as the central
element of *teshuvah*. The key to achieving this, *Igeret
Hateshuvah* explains, is by understanding the G-dly
nature of the human soul and how a person's relationship
with G-d is affected by transgression. This recognition that
G-d is the true essence of our being makes the process
of *teshuvah* relevant for all people, not just transgressors.
Many commentaries have been written on *Igeret
Hateshuvah*. Particularly notable are the many addresses
devoted by the Lubavitcher Rebbe to explaining *Igeret
Hateshuvah*, collected in *Likutei Sichot*, vol. 39.

Rabbi Shneur Zalman of Liadi (1745–1812), known as the
Alter Rebbe, was a Chasidic rebbe, Halachic authority,
and the founder of the Chabad movement. Rabbi Shneur
Zalman was born in Liozna, Belarus, and was among
the principal students of the Magid of Mezeritch. His
works include the *Tanya*, an early classic containing the
fundamentals of Chabad Chasidism; and *Shulchan Aruch
HaRav*, an expanded and reworked code of Jewish law.

Takanat Hashavin

**Rabbi Tzadok Hakohen of Lublin,
Nineteenth Century**
Title page of the first edition of *Takanat
Hashavin*, published in Piotrków, 1926

Takanat Hashavin, by Rabbi Tzadok Hakohen
of Lublin, draws on kabbalah and *Chasidut* to
address the topic of *teshuvah* from an original
perspective. Rabbi Tzadok also discusses the topic
of *teshuvah* in his other works, especially in *Tzidkat
Hatzadik*. He emphasizes recognition of the reality
that even while transgressing, the transgressor
remains connected to G-d; and the power of
teshuvah to retroactively reframe transgressions
as part of a process of spiritual growth.

Rabbi Tzadok Hakohen Rabinowitz of Lublin
(1823–1900) was a Chasidic rebbe and author.
Born into a Lithuanian rabbinic family, Rabbi
Tzadok joined the Chasidic movement and became
a student of Rabbi Mordechai Yosef Leiner of
Izbica and Rabbi Leibel Eiger. He succeeded
Rabbi Eiger after his passing and became a rebbe
in Lublin, Poland. A distinctly original thinker,
Rabbi Tzadok authored many works on Jewish
law, Chasidism, and ethics, as well as scholarly
essays on astronomy, geometry, and algebra.

Orot Hateshuvah

Rabbi Avraham Yitzchak Kook, Twentieth Century

Title page of the first edition of *Orot Hateshuvah*, published in Jerusalem, 1925

Orot Hateshuvah was edited from the writings of Rabbi Avraham Yitzchak Kook by his son, Rabbi Tzvi Yehudah. This work provides an original philosophical and psychological perspective on *teshuvah*. *Orot Hateshuvah* emphasizes *teshuvah* that is performed with joy, analyzes the emotional pain of a remorseful transgressor, and provides guidance and comfort. In addition to addressing personal *teshuvah*, this work discusses national and cosmological *teshuvah*.

Rabbi Avraham Yitzchak Hakohen Kook (1864–1935) was a noted rabbi, author, and thinker. Born in Latvia, Rabbi Kook served as a rabbi in Eastern European communities before immigrating to Israel in 1904 to serve as the rabbi of Jaffa. In 1917, he became the first Ashkenazic chief rabbi of pre-state Israel, and he was a leading figure in the religious Zionist movement. Rabbi Kook wrote many books on Jewish thought and law, including *Orot Hakodesh*, most of which were published posthumously.

Al Hateshuvah

Rabbi Joseph B. Soloveitchik, Twentieth Century

Al Hateshuvah, edited by Dr. Pinchas H. Peli, is based on the lectures of Rabbi Joseph B. Soloveitchik on the concept of *teshuvah*. A new edition of an English translation of this Hebrew work was published by Maggid Books in 2017, under the title, *On Repentance*. In his exploration of *teshuvah*, Rabbi Soloveitchik combines analytical analysis of Halachah, philosophical and theological study of Midrash and Jewish liturgy, and psychological insight into the experiences of the transgressor and penitent. He thereby paints a picture of a "repentant man" defined by profundity of suffering, depth of experience, the ability to exercise free choice, and the capacity to recreate themselves as a new person.

Rabbi Joseph B. Soloveitchik (1903–1993) was a Talmudist, philosopher, and one of the most influential Jewish thinkers and leaders of the twentieth century. A scion of the renowned rabbinic Soloveitchik family of Brisk, Lithuania, he was trained in the "Brisker method" of Talmudic analysis developed by his grandfather, Rabbi Chaim Soloveitchik. He received a PhD in philosophy from the University of Berlin, and was appointed to serve as the rosh yeshiva of RIETS—Yeshiva University, in 1941. His many published works include the multivolume *Shiurei Hagrid* commentary on the Talmud, and the philosophical essay *The Lonely Man of Faith*.

The Jewish Process of Repentance

The following infographics present the concept and process of *teshuvah*, the Jewish process of repentance, along with illustrative and explanatory texts.

YOM TOV DAVENING (PRAYING)
Zalman Kleinman

The Scope of *Teshuvah*

WHO	**Everyone**

MIDRASH

Pirkei Rabbi Eliezer 43

The power of *teshuvah* can be derived from the life story of Rabbi Shimon ben Lakish. In his youth, he patrolled the mountain roads with two comrades. Together, they robbed everyone who crossed their path.

Eventually, he abandoned his two outlaw friends and returned to G-d wholeheartedly, fasting and praying earnestly. He visited the synagogue for prayers each morning and evening, and spent all of his days studying Torah and distributing charity to the needy. He never returned to his negative ways, and G-d accepted his repentance.

FOR WHAT

Everything

WHEN

Anytime

RABBI YOSEF DI TRANI
1568–1639

Based on *Shu"t Maharit, Orach Chayim* 2:8

Inquiry submitted by the judges of a rabbinical court:

Reuben came before us requesting guidance on mending his ways through performing *teshuvah*. When questioned regarding the nature of the transgressions he sought to rectify, he replied that he had committed many serious transgressions—he had completely abandoned Judaism, becoming a bandit who attacked people on the highways, among other serious transgressions. Can such an individual indeed do *teshuvah*? And how might he go about it?

My response:

Indeed, this man has committed extremely grave sins from which it is very difficult to perform *teshuvah*. Nevertheless, if he is truly remorseful and follows the process of *teshuvah* that I will delineate below, nothing will be able to prevent his successful *teshuvah*. G-d extends His hand to transgressors. His right hand stretches forth to receive penitents. Even if an individual has sinned most grievously, G-d accepts their return if they engage in sincere *teshuvah*. No individual is beyond repair.

TALMUD

Based on *Avodah Zarah* 17a

Elazar ben Durdaya had long engaged in a very promiscuous lifestyle when a particular prostitute said to him that even if he were to attempt to repent, G-d would never accept him. This statement shocked him to the core. He pleaded with the mountains and hills, with heaven and earth, with the sun and the moon to pray to their Creator for mercy on his behalf, all to no avail.

Finally, Elazar came to a realization—"This depends on nothing other than me." With his head curled between his knees, he wept and cried loudly until his soul flew from his body. A divine proclamation then rang forth—"Rabbi Elazar ben Durdaya is destined for life in the World to Come."

Five Steps of *Teshuvah*

1   **RESOLUTION**
to not reoffend

2   **REMORSE**
for the offense

**RABBI SHALOM DOVBER SCHNEERSOHN
1860–1920**

The fact that people make excuses for their transgressions is a major problem. Our nature is such that . . . when we do something good we credit ourselves, but when we do something wrong we blame others.

This is a result of self-love. It is our nature to love ourselves, which leads us into denial of our own transgressions, so that we fail to recognize that we are at fault. Even more problematic is the fact that our self-love induces us to create justifications for our negative actions.

It is true that a negative environment and the wrong friends influence us greatly. However, the truth is that we are to blame for choosing to associate with the wrong people and environment. Regardless, it is certainly unacceptable to place the blame only on others, while simultaneously justifying ourselves. . . .

Excusing ourselves by claiming an excitable temperament is similarly not acceptable. Our temperament is a product of our animalistic soul, but we were also given a G-dly soul that provides us with the ability to prevail over our animalistic soul.

This is the very purpose of our creation—to use the power of our G-dly soul to overcome and subdue the inclinations of our animalistic soul. . . . If our animalistic soul is coarse and easily excitable, our G-dly soul surely holds far stronger powers, which provide us with the ability to prevail over our natural inclinations. For G-d does not make demands of us that are beyond our abilities.

Kuntres Umaayan Mibeit Hashem 13:1

③ RESTITUTION

for financial damages

④ APPEASEMENT

of the victim

⑤ VERBAL CONFESSION

to G-d, supported with a verbal statement of remorse for the past and resolution for the future

---

RABBI YEHUDAH LOEW OF PRAGUE
C. 1512–1609

When one individual acts sinfully against another . . . the act has an impact on the victim, who is hurt by the crime. This is the rationale behind the golden rule of repentance: Whenever an offender's behavior negatively impacts a human victim, the offender cannot achieve atonement without appeasing the victim and repairing the damage. Yom Kippur provides an opportunity for atonement only for matters that are between a human and G-d, whereas an injury inflicted upon one human by another cannot be rectified through atonement until the offender seeks forgiveness from the victim.

Derashot HaMaharal MiPrague Derush Al HaTorah,
(Tel Aviv: Yad Mordechai Institute, 1996), p. 47

SEFER HACHINUCH
THIRTEENTH CENTURY

We are commanded to verbally confess our transgressions to G-d. One of the reasons for this is that a verbal expression compels the offender to confront the reality that their actions are fully revealed to G-d, Who knows full well what they have done.

Furthermore, the act of stating the transgression and verbally expressing remorse will cause the offender to be more careful and avoid reoffending in the future.

Sefer Hachinuch, Mitzvah 364

Recommended Post-*Teshuvah* Conduct

 **Increase in prayer.**

Increase in charity.

**Keep a distance from
the circumstances of the
past transgression.**

 **Educate others to avoid
transgression and teach them
about the power of *teshuvah*.**

RABBI ELAZAR OF WORMS
C. 1165–C. 1240

Roke'ach, Laws of Teshuvah 16

Individuals who have stolen from
others and performed *teshuvah*
should be careful to avoid holding
monetary deposits for others or
handling someone else's money. Our
sages taught that "we have a natural
temptation for theft" (Talmud,
Chagigah 11b), so individuals who have
slipped in this regard should distance
themselves from other people's money.
They should engage in charitable
acts—personal deeds of kindness in
addition to distributing money to the
needy—and extend themselves beyond
their means in this pursuit.

RABBI ELAZAR OF WORMS
C. 1165–C. 1240

Yoreh Chata'im 58

A final mission for each returnee is
to inspire others to similarly perform
teshuvah through educating them about
teshuvah and guiding them back to the
correct path. A returnee should caution
others, advising them of the negative
consequences of transgression, and
encourage them by explaining that G-d
will reward them for following the correct
path—and that G-d always accepts those
who return to Him with *teshuvah*. For so
did King David declare while beseeching
G-d regarding his own misdeed—"I will
teach transgressors Your ways, so that they
will return to You" (Psalms 51:15).

JEWISH COMMUNITY
Chaim Leib (Leon) Zernitsky

BEYOND TAKING OFFENSE

You may feel a moral urge to speak up against an offensive action and protect others from harm. But should this translate into a legal responsibility as well? Judaism has a very broad definition of mutual responsibility, and this lesson explores the lengths to which we must go to prevent offenses and protect people from harm.

I. THE QUESTION OF RESPONSIBILITY

This chapter examines the meaning and extent of mutual responsibility: It is natural for members of a society to sense a degree of responsibility toward each other, but are there genuine grounds for such responsibility? And if so, how far does it extend?

As will be demonstrated, Judaism provides a very broad definition of mutual responsibility that emerges from a philosophy of shared purpose, the attribution of high significance to every action, and a spiritual perspective of profound unity between souls.

CASE STUDY A   Chris Dixon and Kevin Sack, "A Friend Lied about Dylann Roof's Massacre Plan. Now He'll Go to Prison," *The New York Times,* March 21, 2017

> Joseph C. Meek Jr., a friend of Dylann S. Roof's who spent time with him in the weeks before nine people were killed at the Emanuel African Methodist Episcopal Church here, was sentenced Tuesday to 27 months in prison for hampering and misleading the federal authorities in the aftermath of Mr. Roof's racist massacre....
>
> Mr. Meek, 22, pleaded guilty last April to two federal counts related to the truthfulness of his responses to the F.B.I. in interviews shortly after the shooting on June 17, 2015 — misprision of a felony and making a false statement to a law enforcement officer. Misprision refers to the failure to report a known crime.

The government did not prosecute Mr. Meek for failing to disclose knowledge of Mr. Roof's plans to attack the church, although it asserted in court filings that his silence "did deprive law enforcement of the opportunity to intervene."

During a night of drinking and drug use about a week before the shootings, Mr. Roof told Mr. Meek that he wanted to kill black people at a historic African Methodist Episcopal church in Charleston in order to start a race riot, according to F.B.I. summaries of interviews with him. Mr. Meek was concerned enough to hide Mr. Roof's handgun after he fell asleep but later returned it and did not report the threat to law enforcement.

"Certainly defendant's failure to make an earlier report is tragic and deeply regrettable, but his failure to report was not a violation of federal criminal law," Judge Gergel wrote last week in an order that denied prosecutors' request to give Mr. Meek a longer term than recommended in sentencing guidelines....

In his initial F.B.I. interview, Mr. Meek denied having known of Mr. Roof's plans and said Mr. Roof had not spoken of a target for his attack, according to Assistant United States Attorney Julius N. Richardson.

But in a second interview, Mr. Meek admitted that he had lied, according to an F.B.I. synopsis of the session. He also admitted that on the night of the shootings, after concluding that Mr. Roof was responsible for the attack, he told others not to contact law enforcement.

Joseph Meek knew of Dylann Roof's intention to commit a massacre and chose not to report it to the authorities who could have prevented it. Despite that, his failure to report a planned crime in advance did not constitute a legal offense. In your opinion, should the act of reporting a plot that involves serious crime be considered:

- commendable
- morally imperative
- a legal obligation

CASE STUDY B   Based on Rabbi Yitzchak Zilberstein, *Chashukei Chemed,* Bava Metzi'a 31a

> Rachel strolls along the street one evening, passing a store that is closed for the night. Glancing through the window, she notices that the air conditioner was left on when it was supposed to be turned off, costing the store owner money. Rachel is unaware of the store owner's identity, but she may be able to receive the owner's contact details from the operators of nearby stores that are still open.

In your opinion, should the effort to alert the storeowner to a costly oversight be considered:

- commendable
- morally imperative
- a legal obligation

RABBI YITZCHAK ZILBERSTEIN 1934–

Expert in areas of Jewish law and medicine. Rabbi Zilberstein is rabbi of the Ramat Elchanan section of Bnei Brak. Born in Poland, he was educated in Jerusalem and married the daughter of Rabbi Yosef Shalom Elyashiv. He is famous for his monthly class on Jewish medical ethics, which is attended by many physicians. He has also published numerous essays on this subject.

CASE STUDY C   Based on Pew Research Center,
"Jewish Americans in 2020," May 11, 2021

Overall, about a quarter of U.S. Jewish adults (27%) do not identify with the Jewish religion: They consider themselves to be Jewish ethnically, culturally, or by family background and have a Jewish parent or were raised Jewish, but they answer a question about their current religion by describing themselves as atheist, agnostic, or "nothing in particular" rather than as Jewish. Among Jewish adults under 30, four-in-ten describe themselves this way. . . .

Among all respondents who indicate they have some kind of Jewish background, those who were raised Jewish by religion have the highest retention rate. Nine-in-ten U.S. adults who were raised Jewish by religion still identify as Jewish today, including 76% who remain Jewish by religion and 13% who are now categorized as Jews of no religion. By comparison, three-quarters of those raised as Jews of no religion still identify as Jewish today; roughly half are still Jews of no religion and about one-in-five are now Jewish by religion. Among those who had at least one Jewish parent but who say they were not raised exclusively Jewish (either by religion or aside from religion), far fewer identify as Jewish today (29%).

FIGURE 3.1

Jewish Identity in the United States, 2020

Pew Research Center, "Jewish Americans in 2020"

U.S. Jewish Identity, by Age

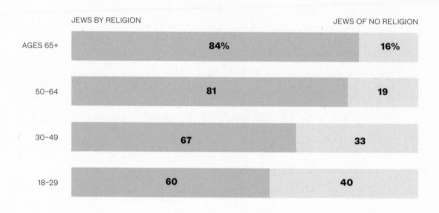

JEWS BY RELIGION   JEWS OF NO RELIGION

AGES 65+	84%	16%
50-64	81	19
30-49	67	33
18-29	60	40

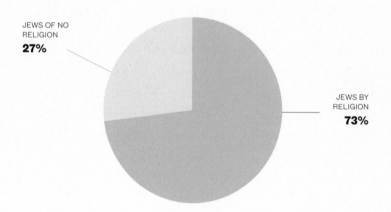

JEWS OF NO RELIGION
27%

JEWS BY RELIGION
73%

Nine-in-ten Americans raised Jewish by religion and three-quarters raised as Jews of no religion continue to identify as Jewish

Among U.S. adults who were raised Jewish or had at least one Jewish parent

% who today:	All	Raised Jewish by religion	Raised Jewish of no religion	Not raised exclusively Jewish, but had Jewish parent(s)
	%	%	%	%
Identify as Jewish	**68**	**90**	**76**	**29**
Jews by religion	49	76	21	8
Jews of no religion	19	13	54	22
Do not identify as Jewish	**32**	**10**	**24**	**71**
	100	**100**	**100**	**100**

These numbers depict American Jewry in a state of serious decline, with Jewish identity on a weakening trend.

1.   What should we do to reverse the trend of weakening Jewish identity?

2.   Is someone else's degree of religious observance or Jewish identity any business of ours?

   Yes   No

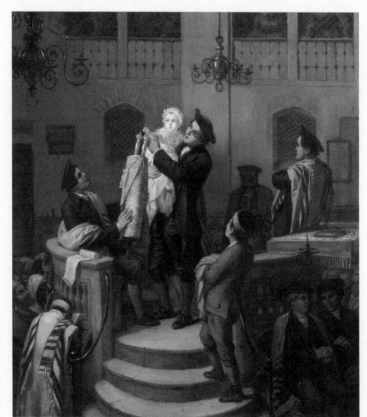

DAS SCHULTRAGEN—THE PRESENTATION AT THE SYNAGOGUE

Moritz Daniel Oppenheim (1800–1882), oil on canvas, 1869. (The Jewish Museum, New York) This scene depicts a custom specific to German Jews in which a decorated Torah binder made from material used at a baby's circumcision is donated to the synagogue upon the boy's first visit.

TEXT 1

Acceptance of the Torah

Exodus 19:8

וַיַּעֲנוּ כָל הָעָם יַחְדָּו וַיֹּאמְרוּ, כֹּל אֲשֶׁר דִּבֶּר ה' נַעֲשֶׂה.

The people all responded in unison,
"We will do everything G-d has said."

Moses receiving the law with Aaron and the Israelites waiting behind him at the foot of the mountain. Initial word panel from the second volume of the Tripartite Machzor, a three volume prayer book created in Germany c. 1322. The scribe is named Chaim, although more information about him is unknown. This beautiful manuscript contains many richly decorated miniatures, initial word panels, and medallions. (British Library, London [MS 22413])

TEXT 2

Joyful Guarantee

Midrash, *Tanchuma* 19:13

בְּשָׁעָה שֶׁעָמְדוּ יִשְׂרָאֵל עַל הַר סִינַי, הִשְׁווּ כּוּלָן לֵב אֶחָד לְקַבֵּל עֲלֵיהֶם מַלְכוּת שָׁמַיִם בְּשִׂמְחָה, שֶׁנֶּאֱמַר, וַיַּעֲנוּ כָל הָעָם יַחְדָּו וַיֹּאמְרוּ (שְׁמוֹת יט, ח). וְלֹא עוֹד, אֶלָּא שֶׁהָיוּ מְמַשְׁכְּנִין עַצְמָן זֶה עַל זֶה.

When the Jewish people accepted G-d's rule at Mount Sinai, they did so joyfully, as one, as the verse states, "The people all responded in unison" (EXODUS 19:8). In doing so, they even committed to serving as guarantors for each other.

TANCHUMA

A Midrashic work bearing the name of Rabbi Tanchuma, a 4th-century Talmudic sage quoted often in this work. "Midrash" is the designation of a particular genre of rabbinic literature usually forming a running commentary on specific books of the Bible. *Tanchuma* provides textual exegeses, expounds upon the biblical narrative, and develops and illustrates moral principles. *Tanchuma* is unique in that many of its sections commence with a Halachic discussion, which subsequently leads into nonhalachic teachings.

SIMCHAT TORAH CELEBRATION
Alex Levin, oil on canvas, 2020

Watch **Rabbi Adin Even-Israel (Steinsaltz)** discuss how Torah study can foster Jewish unity: **myjli.com/beyondright**

TEXT 3

On the Same Boat

Midrash, *Eliyahu Rabah* 11

TANA DEVEI ELIYAHU

A Midrashic work,
sometimes referred to as
Seder Eliyahu. Midrash
is the designation of
a particular genre of
rabbinic literature
usually forming a
running commentary
on specific books of the
Bible. This work deals
with the divine precepts,
their rationales, and the
importance of knowledge
of Torah, prayer, and
repentance. The work is
divided into 2 sections
(*sedarim*): *Eliyahu
Rabah* and *Eliyahu Zuta*.

כָּל יִשְׂרָאֵל עֲרֵבִים זֶה לָזֶה. וּלְמָה הֵן דוֹמִים,
לִסְפִינָה שֶׁנִּקְרַע בָּהּ בַּיִת אֶחָד. אֵין אוֹמְרִים נִקְרַע
בָּהּ בַּיִת אֶחָד, אֶלָא כָּל הַסְּפִינָה נִקְרְעָה כֻּלָּה.

All Jews are mutually responsible. This can
be compared to a ship where a hole has
been ruptured in one of its cabins. We do
not exclaim, "A cabin has ruptured!" Rather,
we say, "The entire ship is ruptured!"

TEXT 4

The Power of Every Action

Maimonides, *Mishneh Torah*, Laws of *Teshuvah* 3:4

**RABBI MOSHE BEN MAIMON
(MAIMONIDES, RAMBAM)
1135–1204**

Halachist, philosopher, author,
and physician. Maimonides
was born in Córdoba, Spain.
After the conquest of Córdoba
by the Almohads, he fled
Spain and eventually settled
in Cairo, Egypt. There, he
became the leader of the
Jewish community and served
as court physician to the vizier
of Egypt. He is most noted
for authoring the *Mishneh
Torah*, an encyclopedic
arrangement of Jewish law;
and for his philosophical
work, *Guide for the Perplexed*.
His rulings on Jewish law
are integral to the formation
of Halachic consensus.

צָרִיךְ כָּל אָדָם שֶׁיִּרְאֶה עַצְמוֹ כָּל הַשָּׁנָה כֻּלָּה כְּאִלּוּ חֶצְיוֹ
זַכַּאי וְחֶצְיוֹ חַיָּב, וְכֵן כָּל הָעוֹלָם, חֶצְיוֹ זַכַּאי וְחֶצְיוֹ חַיָּב.

חָטָא חֵטְא אֶחָד, הֲרֵי הִכְרִיעַ עַצְמוֹ וְהִכְרִיעַ אֶת
כָּל הָעוֹלָם כֻּלּוֹ לְכַף חוֹבָה, וְגָרַם לָהֶן הַשְׁחָתָה.

עָשָׂה מִצְוָה אַחַת, הֲרֵי הִכְרִיעַ אֶת עַצְמוֹ וְהִכְרִיעַ אֶת
כָּל הָעוֹלָם כֻּלּוֹ לְכַף זְכוּת, וְגָרַם לָהֶן תְּשׁוּעָה וְהַצָּלָה.

זֶה הוּא שֶׁנֶּאֱמַר, "וְצַדִּיק יְסוֹד עוֹלָם" (מִשְׁלֵי י, כה),
זֶה שֶׁצִּדֵּק עַצְמוֹ הִכְרִיעַ אֶת כָּל הָעוֹלָם כֻּלּוֹ וְהִצִּילוֹ.

We should always consider ourselves, and the entire world, as equally balanced between merit and guilt.

If we perform one transgression, we may tip our personal balance, and that of the entire world, to the side of guilt, and we bring destruction upon everyone.

Conversely, if we perform one mitzvah, we may tip our balance, and that of the entire world, to the side of merit, bringing deliverance and salvation to all.

This dynamic is reflected in the verse, "A righteous person is the foundation of the world" (PROVERBS 10:25), meaning that a person who acts righteously tips the balance of the entire world and saves it.

The Worms Machzor, a 2-volume prayerbook for the festivals, written according to the Ashkenazi rite, endured many trials following its creation in Wurzburg, Germany, in the late 13th century. After the destruction of the community in Wurzburg during the Rindfleisch persecution, the Machzor was most likely brought to Worms, Germany, by refugees, where it was used until the synagogue's destruction on Kristallnacht in November of 1938. The book was rescued and hidden by the city's archivist, and it was finally transferred to the Jewish National and University Library of Jerusalem in 1957. The illumination here depicts a man holding a scale. As Maimonides explains each person must view himself as having the ability, through a single action, to tip the balance of the world either to the side of guilt and destruction, or to merit and salvation.

TEXT 5

Soulful Unity

Rabbi Moshe Cordovero, *Tomer Devorah* 1

RABBI
MOSHE CORDOVERO
(RAMAK)
1522–1570

כָּל יִשְׂרָאֵל הֵם שְׁאֵר בָּשָׂר אֵלּוּ עִם אֵלּוּ מִפְּנֵי שֶׁהַנְּשָׁמוֹת
כְּלוּלוֹת יַחַד, יֵשׁ בָּזֶה חֵלֶק זֶה וּבָזֶה חֵלֶק זֶה . . .

וְכֵן מִטַּעַם זֶה יִשְׂרָאֵל עֲרֵבִים זֶה לָזֶה, מִפְּנֵי שֶׁמַּמָּשׁ
יֵשׁ בְּכָל אֶחָד חֵלֶק אֶחָד מֵחֲבֵרוֹ. וּכְשֶׁחוֹטֵא הָאֶחָד,
פּוֹגֵם אֶת עַצְמוֹ וּפוֹגֵם חֵלֶק אֲשֶׁר לַחֲבֵרוֹ בּוֹ . . .

וּלְכָךְ רָאוּי לְאָדָם לִהְיוֹתוֹ חָפֵץ בְּטוֹבָתוֹ שֶׁל חֲבֵרוֹ,
וְעֵינוֹ טוֹבָה עַל טוֹבַת חֲבֵרוֹ, וּכְבוֹדוֹ יִהְיֶה חָבִיב
עָלָיו כְּשֶׁלּוֹ, שֶׁהֲרֵי הוּא הוּא מַמָּשׁ. וּמִטַּעַם זֶה
נִצְטַוִּינוּ, "וְאָהַבְתָּ לְרֵעֲךָ כָּמוֹךָ" (וַיִקְרָא יט, יח).

All Jews are interrelated because our
souls are commingled, and we each
share a part of each other's soul. . . .

This is why all Jews bear mutual responsibility—we
each possess an actual spiritual part of our fellow. As a
result, when one Jew transgresses, their action causes
damage to themselves and inflicts damage to the
part of them that is shared by their fellow Jews. . . .

Join **Rabbi Laibl
Wolf** for a guided
meditation about
Jewish love and unity:
myjli.com/beyondright

Therefore, we should all seek out each other's benefit,
rejoice in each other's success, and respect our fellow
Jew as we respect ourselves—because we really are
one. This is the basis for the commandment to "love
your fellow as yourself" (LEVITICUS 19:18).

Prominent kabbalist.
Ramak belonged to the
circle of Jewish mystical
thinkers who flourished
in 16th-century Safed.
The name Cordovero
indicates that his family
originated in Córdoba,
Spain. His most famous
kabbalistic work is
Pardes Rimonim.

II. LIFE AND LIVELIHOOD

After studying the philosophical underpinnings of the Jewish value of mutual responsibility, we now proceed to explore how this value is expressed in Jewish law. We begin with the issue of our responsibility to prevent harm to others' lives and property.

Illegal Bystanding

Leviticus 19:16

לֹא תַעֲמֹד עַל דַּם רֵעֶךָ.

Do not stand by the shedding of your fellow's blood.

Active Intervention

Maimonides, *Sefer Hamitzvot*, negative commandment 297

הִזְהִירָנוּ מִלְּהִתְרַשֵּׁל בְּהַצָּלַת נֶפֶשׁ אֶחָד כְּשֶׁנִּרְאֵהוּ
בְּסַכָּנַת מָוֶת אוֹ הֶהֶפְסֵד וְיִהְיֶה לָנוּ יְכֹלֶת לְהַצִּילוֹ.
כְּמוֹ שֶׁהָיָה טוֹבֵעַ בַּנָּהָר וַאֲנַחְנוּ נֵדַע לִשְׂחוֹת וְנוּכַל
לְהַצִּילוֹ, אוֹ יִהְיֶה לִסְטִים מִשְׁתַּדֵּל לְהָרְגוֹ וְנוּכַל לְבַטֵּל
מַחֲשַׁבְתּוֹ אוֹ לִדְחוֹת מִמֶּנּוּ נֵזֶק. וּבָאָה הָאַזְהָרָה
בְּאָמְרוֹ, לֹא תַעֲמֹד עַל דַּם רֵעֶךָ (ויקרא יט, טז).

This prohibition forbids us to refrain from intervening to save others when we see that they are in danger of death or financial loss and we have the ability to rescue them: for example, if someone is drowning in the sea and we are able to swim out and save him; or if robbers are planning to kill someone and we are able to dissuade the plotters or protect the victim from harm. Regarding all such cases, we are commanded, "Do not stand by the shedding of your fellow's blood" (LEVITICUS 19:16).

TEXT 7

Returning Lost Items

Deuteronomy 22:1–3

לֹא תִרְאֶה אֶת שׁוֹר אָחִיךָ אוֹ אֶת שֵׂיוֹ נִדָּחִים
וְהִתְעַלַּמְתָּ מֵהֶם, הָשֵׁב תְּשִׁיבֵם לְאָחִיךָ . . .
וְכֵן תַּעֲשֶׂה לְכָל אֲבֵדַת אָחִיךָ.

You shall not witness your fellow's ox or sheep straying and ignore them. Rather, you must return them to your fellow. . . . So must you do with anything lost by your fellow.

Preventing Loss

Talmud, Bava Metzi'a 31a

אָמַר רָבָא, לְכָל אֲבֵידַת אָחִיךָ
(דְּבָרִים כב, ג), לְרַבּוֹת אֲבֵידַת קַרְקַע.

אָמַר לֵיה רַב חֲנַנְיָה לְרָבָא, תַּנְיָא דִמְסַיֵּיע לָךְ:
רָאָה מַיִם שֶׁשּׁוֹטְפִין וּבָאִין, הֲרֵי זֶה גּוֹדֵר בִּפְנֵיהֶם.

Rava taught: The verse states, "So must you do with *anything* belonging to your fellow" (DEUTERONOMY 22:3). The mention of "anything" comes to include preventing damage to someone else's property.

Rabbi Chananyah said to Rava, "There is an earlier teaching that supports your ruling: 'If you observe floodwater advancing toward your fellow's field, you must erect a barrier to protect the field.'"

BABYLONIAN TALMUD

A literary work of monumental proportions that draws upon the legal, spiritual, intellectual, ethical, and historical traditions of Judaism. The 37 tractates of the Babylonian Talmud contain the teachings of the Jewish sages from the period after the destruction of the 2nd Temple through the 5th century CE. It has served as the primary vehicle for the transmission of the Oral Law and the education of Jews over the centuries; it is the entry point for all subsequent legal, ethical, and theological Jewish scholarship.

This illustration of the Israelites walking on dry land between the Egyptian army drowning at sea is one of the many rich decorations in the Rylands *Haggadah*. This parchment manuscript, created in Catalonia, Spain, in the mid-14th century, contains many beautiful paintings, initial word panels, micrography, and decorations related to the Passover story and liturgy. (The John Rylands Library, The University of Manchester Library [Hebrew MS 6])

TEXT 9

A Question of Precedence

Talmud, Bava Metzi'a 33a

אֲבֵדָתוֹ וַאֲבֵדַת אָבִיו, אֲבֵדָתוֹ קוֹדֶמֶת. אֲבֵדָתוֹ וַאֲבֵדַת
רַבּוֹ, שֶׁלוֹ קֹדֶם . . . שֶׁלְּךָ קֹדֶם לְשֶׁל כָּל אָדָם.

מְנָא הַנֵּי מִילֵּי, אָמַר רַב יְהוּדָה אָמַר רַב אָמַר קְרָא אֶפֶס כִּי
לֹא יִהְיֶה בְּךָ אֶבְיוֹן (דְּבָרִים טו, ד). שֶׁלְּךָ קוֹדֶם לְשֶׁל כָּל אָדָם.

וְאָמַר רַב יְהוּדָה אָמַר רַב, כָּל הַמְקַיֵּם
בְּעַצְמוֹ כָּךְ סוֹף בָּא לִידֵי כָּךְ.

If you find your own lost object alongside your father's lost object, retrieving your personal asset takes precedence. If you encounter your own lost object alongside your teacher's, your personal asset takes precedence.... Your assets take precedence over those of anyone else.

From where is this law derived? Rabbi Yehudah quoted Rav: The verse states, "so that there should be no impoverished among you" (DEUTERONOMY 15:4). You must avoid becoming impoverished, so your assets take precedence over the assets of anyone else.

However, Rabbi Yehudah quoted a warning issued by Rav: "People who are strict in their application of this principle will eventually meet the impoverished state they are seeking to avoid."

TEXT 10

Making Every Effort

Rabbi Shneur Zalman of Liadi, *Shulchan Aruch HaRav,*
Choshen Mishpat, Laws Pertaining to Lost Items and Deposits 37

**RABBI SHNEUR
ZALMAN OF LIADI
(ALTER REBBE)
1745–1812**

Chasidic rebbe, Halachic
authority, and founder of
the Chabad movement.
The Alter Rebbe was
born in Liozna, Belarus,
and was among the
principal students of the
Magid of Mezeritch. His
numerous works include
the *Tanya,* an early
classic containing the
fundamentals of Chabad
Chasidism; and *Shulchan
Aruch HaRav,* an
expanded and reworked
code of Jewish law.

אִם לֹא הָיָה מַחְזִירָם לְעַצְמוֹ מֵחֲמַת הַטֹּרַח, שֶׁלֹּא
הָיָה חָפֵץ לִטְרֹחַ לִשָּׂא אוֹתָם לְבֵיתוֹ הוֹאִיל וְהֵם
כֵּלִים פְּחוּתִים וּדְמֵיהֶם מוּעָטִים . . . חַיָּב מִן הַדִּין
לִטְרֹחַ בָּהֶם עַד שֶׁיַּגִּיעוּ לִרְשׁוּת הַבְּעָלִים.

כִּי בְּשֶׁלּוֹ הוּא רַשַּׁאי לְוַתֵּר עַל מָמוֹנוֹ מִפְּנֵי טֹרַח גּוּפוֹ
וְלֹא בְּשֶׁל חֲבֵרוֹ. שֶׁהַתּוֹרָה לֹא חָסָה . . . עַל טֹרַח הַגּוּף
אֲפִלּוּ טֹרַח מְרֻבֶּה מְאֹד עַל שְׁוֶה פְּרוּטָה אַחַת.

If we encounter lost items of insignificant value,
to the point that if they were our own, we would
not bother to collect them and take them home . . .
we are nevertheless obligated to make the
necessary effort to restore them to their owner.

The rationale is that we have the right to relinquish
our possessions if their value is outweighed by the
physical burden they impose. However, we have
no right to unilaterally relinquish someone else's
ownership over their possessions. The Torah does
not allow us to spare any effort, even if the effort
is great and the value of the item is minimal.

TEXT 11

The Price of Inaction

Tosefta, Shevu'ot 3:2

יוֹדֵעַ עֵדוּת לַחֲבֵרוֹ וְאֵינוֹ מֵעִיד, אֵינוֹ חַיָּב לְשַׁלֵּם מִן הַדִּין.

וְאֵין הַשָּׁמַיִם מוֹחֲלִים לוֹ עַד שֶׁיְשַׁלֵּם.

Those who could rightly testify for someone but fail to do so are not legally liable to provide compensation for the damage they could have prevented.

However, such people will not be granted divine forgiveness until they pay for the damage.

TOSEFTA

A compendium of laws similar in format to that of the Mishnah; it consists of teachings of the sages of the Mishnah. At times, the material in both works is similar; at other times, there are significant differences between the two. The Talmud often compares these texts in its analysis. According to tradition, the *Tosefta* was redacted by Rabbis Chiyah and Oshiyah in the beginning of the 3rd century in the Land of Israel.

Copied in Germany during the 12th century, the Erfurt Manuscript is the oldest known manuscript of the *Tosefta*. It is incomplete and seems to have not been finished by the scribe. The final page contains a partial recount of its history, which continues in the memorial book of the city of Erfurt, Germany. Bloodstains on the manuscript and its 1879 location in the Erfurt Evangelical Church suggest that it might have been violently taken during a pogrom and placed there together with other stolen Jewish manuscripts. The collection was transferred to the German National Library, where it remains until today. (Berlin National Library [*Tosefta* Ms Erfurt 12])

III. MITZVAH RESPONSIBILITY

In addition to caring for each other's material welfare, the Jewish value of mutual responsibility also manifests itself in the realm of spiritual welfare. We are called upon to guide others away from transgressing the Torah's prohibitions and to assist them in observing the *mitzvot*.

TEXT 12

Giving Critique

Leviticus 19:17

הוֹכֵחַ תּוֹכִיחַ אֶת עֲמִיתֶךָ וְלֹא תִשָּׂא עָלָיו חֵטְא.

You shall surely critique your fellow and you will not share in their guilt.

TEXT 13

What's My Business?

Maimonides, *Sefer Hamitzvot*, positive mitzvah 205

וְאַל יֹאמַר אָדָם, אֲנִי לֹא אֶחֱטָא, וְאִם יֶחֱטָא זוּלָתִי, זֶה עִנְיָינוֹ עִם ה'. זֶה נֶגֶד הַתּוֹרָה. אֶלָּא אָנוּ מְצֻוִּוים שֶׁלֹּא נַעֲבוֹר וְלֹא נָנִיחַ לְזוּלָתֵנוּ מֵאֻמָּתֵנוּ לַעֲבוֹר.

One should not say, "I will act righteously, and if others choose to stray from the path of righteousness, that is a matter that is between them and G-d." This attitude is antithetical to Torah values. Rather, we are commanded to do the right thing ourselves, and to see to it that others, too, conduct themselves appropriately.

TEXT 14

How to Critique

Maimonides, *Mishneh Torah*, Laws of Personal Development 6:7

הַמּוֹכִיחַ אֶת חֲבֵרוֹ, בֵּין בִּדְבָרִים שֶׁבֵּינוֹ לְבֵינוֹ בֵּין בִּדְבָרִים
שֶׁבֵּינוֹ לְבֵין הַמָּקוֹם, צָרִיךְ לְהוֹכִיחוֹ בֵּינוֹ לְבֵין עַצְמוֹ.
וִידַבֵּר לוֹ בְּנַחַת וּבְלָשׁוֹן רַכָּה, וְיוֹדִיעוֹ שֶׁאֵינוֹ אוֹמֵר
לוֹ אֶלָּא לְטוֹבָתוֹ, וְלַהֲבִיאוֹ לְחַיֵּי הָעוֹלָם הַבָּא.

When we critique others—whether regarding
an interpersonal issue or a religious matter—it
should be done in private. We must speak
patiently and gently, clarifying that we are
motivated solely by their welfare and our desire
that they merit reward in the World to Come.

TEXT 15

Assuming Permission

Rabbi Shneur Zalman of Liadi, *Shulchan Aruch HaRav,
Orach Chayim* 586:5

מֻתָּר לִטֹּל שׁוֹפָר שֶׁל חֲבֵרוֹ שֶׁלֹּא מִדַּעְתּוֹ לִתְקֹעַ
בּוֹ תְּקִיעָה שֶׁל מִצְוָה . . . דְּמִן הַסְּתָם נוֹחַ לוֹ לָאָדָם
שֶׁיַּעֲשׂוּ מִצְוָה בְּמָמוֹנוֹ בְּדָבָר שֶׁאֵין בּוֹ חֶסְרוֹן כִּיס.

It is permissible to use someone else's shofar without
advance permission in order to fulfill the mitzvah. . . .
We assume that people would happily oblige
others to perform a mitzvah with their possessions,
provided that no financial loss is incurred as a result.

TEXT 16

Template for Mitzvah Blessings

Siddur

בָּרוּךְ אַתָּה ה' אֱלֹקֵינוּ מֶלֶךְ הָעוֹלָם
אֲשֶׁר קִדְּשָׁנוּ בְּמִצְוֹתָיו וְצִוָּנוּ . . .

Blessed are You, G-d our L-rd, King of the universe, who sanctified us with His commandments and commanded us concerning . . .

SIDDUR

The siddur is the Jewish prayer book. It was originally developed by the sages of the Great Assembly in the 4th century BCE and later reconstructed by Rabban Gamliel after the destruction of the Second Temple. Various authorities continued to add prayers, from then until contemporary times. It includes praise of G-d, requests for personal and national needs, selections from the Bible, and much else. Various Jewish communities have slightly different versions of the siddur.

An illustration of a woman lighting Shabbat candles followed by a prayer and the text of the blessing. This decorated manuscript by Aaron Wolf Herlingen, created in 1736, contains selected prayers, blessings, and liturgy in a combination common to the time period. (Library of the JTS, New York [MS 4789])

TEXT 17

Acting on Others' Behalf

Mishnah, Rosh Hashanah 3:8

זֶה הַכְּלָל, כָּל שֶׁאֵינוֹ מְחָיָב בַּדָּבָר אֵינוֹ
מוֹצִיא אֶת הָרַבִּים יְדֵי חוֹבָתָן.

This is the rule: whoever is not personally obligated in a particular mitzvah cannot perform it on behalf of others.

TEXT 18

Blessing for Others

Talmud, Rosh Hashanah 29a

כָּל הַבְּרָכוֹת כֻּלָּן, אַף עַל פִּי שֶׁיָּצָא, מוֹצִיא.

With regard to all blessings, the rule is that people who have fulfilled their own obligation can nevertheless repeat it for the sake of causing others to fulfill their obligation.

MISHNAH

The first authoritative work of Jewish law that was codified in writing. The Mishnah contains the oral traditions that were passed down from teacher to student; it supplements, clarifies, and systematizes the commandments of the Torah. Due to the continual persecution of the Jewish people, it became increasingly difficult to guarantee that these traditions would not be forgotten. Rabbi Yehudah Hanasi therefore redacted the Mishnah at the end of the 2nd century. It serves as the foundation for the Talmud.

Your Lack Is My Lack

TEXT 19

Rabbi Nisim of Gerona, Rosh Hashanah 29a

RABBI NISIM BEN REUVEN
"THE RAN" OF GERONA
1320–1380

Influential talmudist
and authority on Jewish
law; among the last
great Spanish Talmudic
scholars. Considered
the outstanding
Halachic authority of his
generation, queries came
to him from throughout
the Diaspora. His works
include commentaries
on the Talmud and on
Rabbi Yitzchak Alfasi's
code, responsa literature,
a commentary on the
Bible, and a collection
of sermons, *Derashot
HaRan*, which elucidates
fundamentals of Judaism.

שֶׁהֲרֵי כָּל יִשְׂרָאֵל עֲרֵבִין זֶה בָּזֶה לְמִצְוֹת,
וְכֵיוָן שֶׁלֹא יָצָא חֲבֵרוֹ כְּמִי שֶׁלֹא יָצָא הוּא דָמִי.

The reason for this law is that all Jews are
responsible for each other in mitzvah-related
matters. Consequently, if my fellow hasn't yet
fulfilled their mitzvah obligation, I haven't
completely fulfilled my own obligation either.

EXERCISE 3.1

**How can I better apply the Jewish value of mutual
responsibility in my personal life?**

In this address, **the
Lubavitcher Rebbe**
passionately speaks about
our love and responsibility
for our fellow Jews:
myjli.com/beyondright

KEY POINTS

1 Judaism has a very broad definition of mutual responsibility, based on a vision of shared purpose and mission, which is influenced by each action of every person.

2 In addition to a shared mission, Jewish mysticism teaches that our souls are united.

3 Jewish law considers it a crime to remain silent when aware of a threat to someone else's life, and it also mandates that we extend every effort necessary to protect others from monetary loss.

4 The Jewish value of mutual responsibility calls on us to guide others away from transgression of the Torah's commandments. This must be done gently, and be motivated by genuine concern for their spiritual welfare.

5 Jewish law also teaches that we are responsible to assist others in the performance of *mitzvot*. Our own mitzvah observance is incomplete until we do so.

The Rebbe's Ten-Point Mitzvah Campaign

The word mitzvah, "commandment," also means "connection." It refers to an act that *connects* the individual who accomplishes the deed with G-d, the Giver of the commandment. Beyond obligations, *mitzvot* are *opportunities* to forge the ultimate connection to which a mortal can aspire.

For this reason, the Lubavitcher Rebbe powerfully highlighted the infinite value of a single mitzvah performance, independent of an individual's commitment to Jewish practice or lack thereof.

To provide each Jew with an opportunity to connect, the Rebbe identified ten "beginner's *mitzvot*"—ten precepts whose centrality to Judaism make each of them ideally suited for a first or stand-alone experience of the connection. The Rebbe turned these into ten global mitzvah campaigns that continue to transform the Jewish world.

① TEFILIN

Men and boys (aged thirteen and up) should wear *tefilin* each morning, excluding Shabbat and Jewish festivals. The *tefilin*'s black leather boxes contain small parchment scrolls bearing selected portions from the Torah that deliver the fundamentals of Jewish faith and practice.

② TZEDAKAH

Ideally, each Jew should donate to charity (*tzedakah*) daily. In assisting those in need, we become G-d's ambassadors and partners to provide for G-d's creations. Each Jewish home should contain a prominently placed charity box, and its household members should be encouraged to donate on a regular basis.

③ TORAH STUDY

Jews should study Torah—daily. It's a soul's oxygen. Even a few lines contain G-d's infinite wisdom and will, so that a minimum of study yields a powerful connection. The more substantial the study, the richer the bond.

④ A HOUSE FILLED WITH JEWISH BOOKS

A Jewish home needs Jewish furniture. Furnish your home with as many holy Jewish texts as possible. At a minimum, you should have these three for your spirit to feel at home: *Chumash* (Jewish Bible), Tehilim (Hebrew Psalms), and siddur (Jewish prayer book).

⑤ *MEZUZAH*

A Jewish home should have a *mezuzah* affixed to the doorpost of each doorway. This is a miniature parchment scroll (placed in a case) bearing the *Shema*—a Torah passage that includes Judaism's ultimate declaration of faith. It serves as a sign that G-d's presence is welcome in the home and it elicits G-d's overt protection over the property and its inhabitants.

⑥ SHABBAT CANDLES

Women and girls (aged three and up) should kindle Shabbat lights every Friday afternoon. This beautiful ritual is performed eighteen minutes *before* sunset in honor of the imminent arrival of Shabbat. Lights are also kindled to usher in the Jewish festivals and holy days.

⑦ FAMILY PURITY

The Torah provides a body of divine guidance for sanctifying marriage, allowing couples to merge and new humans to be produced amid soulful sanctity, new depths of intimacy, and a pure, powerful, loving, and lasting relationship.

⑧ KOSHER

For a Jewish soul to thrive, its body needs a kosher diet. Observing the laws of *kashrut* (keeping kosher) is an indispensable way to make our souls shine.

⑨ JEWISH EDUCATION

Each Jewish child—girl or boy—needs a Jewish education, for their own Jewish present and future, and to guarantee the future of the Jewish people and their divine mission.

⑩ LOVE YOUR FELLOW

The Torah tells us to "love your fellow as yourself." Rabbi Akiva, a master sage of the Talmudic era, identified this call as a fundamental principle of the Torah. We all need to relate to our fellow Jews with enhanced love, care, and concern—just as we care deeply about ourselves. After all, as living branches of an indivisible and eternal divine entity, all Jews are one.

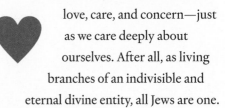

4

BEYOND PERSONAL FREEDOM

*With 613 commandments in the Torah and myriad
rules expounded in the Talmud, can Judaism ever be
called "liberating"? In this lesson we delve into the
Exodus and the Covenant at Mount Sinai for a new
definition of freedom, and then we explore how the
value of personal liberty guides Jewish law about the
employer-employee relationship.*

I. THE MEANING OF FREEDOM

Freedom is a value we all cherish. This study explores the Jewish perspective on what freedom really means, and the ways in which this Jewish value of freedom finds expression in practical Jewish law.

The opening text takes us back to the mid-nineteenth century, when slavery was still the law of the land in numerous American states.

TEXT 1

Betty's Case

Justice Lemuel Shaw, "Betty's Case," Massachusetts Supreme Judicial Court, 20 *Monthly Law Reporter*, pp. 455–458 (Nov. 9, 1857)

LEMUEL SHAW
1781–1861

A native of Massachusetts, Lemuel Shaw was a prominent lawyer in Boston before his election to the Massachusetts House of Representatives and State Senate. In 1830 Shaw was appointed chief justice of the Massachusetts Supreme Judicial Court, a position he held for the next 30 years. He is known for his rulings on prominent cases involving slavery, segregation, and religion.

Habeas corpus upon petition of Lucy S. Schuyler, of Lawrence, setting forth that a colored woman, named Betty, was restrained of her liberty, at said Lawrence, by Sullivan Sweet and his wife. After the writ had been read, the counsel for the respondents stated that they belonged in Tennessee, and had been travelling with their servant Betty, in Canada and several of the Northern States, and for the last six weeks had been at Lawrence. That Betty had, during all this time, been aware that she was entitled to her liberty, and had been under no restraint; and that his clients were willing to abide by her choice. . . .

Whereupon, I proposed and had an examination of the said Betty apart from the said Sweet and wife, and all other persons—upon which it appeared to me, that she is twenty-five years old, intelligent and capable of judging for herself; that she has a husband in Tennessee and other relatives; that she is much attached to Mr. and Mrs. Sweet; is very well treated by them, and desires to remain and return with them, and this desire she expressed decisively and upon repeated inquiries. I explained to her her right to freedom and protection here, and that she could not lawfully be taken away against her will. . . .

Now it was contrary to all the principles of freedom that this or any other person should not exercise a free choice in such a matter. Betty was entirely at liberty to exercise her free choice, and no one could interfere with her, without incurring a personal liability. . . .

Whereupon it was ordered and adjudged, that the said Betty be at free liberty to remain with Mr. and Mrs. Sweet, or go elsewhere, at her free choice, and that all persons be interdicted and forbidden to interfere with her personal liberty in this respect.

QUESTION

In your opinion, should a person be free to choose to be a slave?

Yes   No

Two Theories of Freedom

Ian Carter, "Positive and Negative Liberty," *The Stanford Encyclopedia of Philosophy* (Winter 2019 Edition), Edward N. Zalta (ed.)

IAN CARTER, PHD

Political theorist. Dr. Carter is associate professor of political philosophy at University of Pavia, Italy. His research focuses on ideas such as freedom, rights, and equality in contemporary political philosophy. He is the author of *A Measure of Freedom*.

Negative liberty is the absence of obstacles, barriers or constraints. One has negative liberty to the extent that actions are available to one in this negative sense. Positive liberty is the possibility of acting—or the fact of acting—in such a way as to take control of one's life and realize one's fundamental purposes. . . . The idea of distinguishing between a negative and a positive sense of the term 'liberty' goes back at least to Kant, and was examined and defended in depth by Isaiah Berlin in the 1950s and '60s.

Rabbi Aryeh Weinstein discusses different forms of freedom: **myjli.com/beyondright**

The Liberty Bell, in Philadelphia, is inscribed with a quote from Leviticus 25:10: "Proclaim liberty throughout all the land unto all the inhabitants thereof."

1. Which of these definitions of freedom resonates more with you?

   ○ Negative Liberty   ○ Positive Liberty

2. Why?

3. Based on the *negative* definition of freedom, should an individual be free to choose to be a slave?

   ○ Yes ○ No

4. Based on the *positive* definition of freedom, should an individual be free to choose to be a slave?

   ○ Yes ○ No

TEXT 3

Torah Freedom

Avot 6:2

אֵין לְךָ בֶּן חוֹרִין
אֶלָּא מִי שֶׁעוֹסֵק בַּתּוֹרָה.

No person is free except for those who
occupy themselves with Torah.

**AVOT
(ETHICS OF THE
FATHERS; PIRKEI AVOT)**

A 6-chapter work on
Jewish ethics that is
studied widely by Jewish
communities, especially
during the summer. The
first 5 chapters are from
the Mishnah, tractate
Avot. Avot differs from
the rest of the Mishnah
in that it does not focus
on legal subjects; it
is a collection of the
sages' wisdom on topics
related to character
development, ethics,
healthy living, piety, and
the study of Torah.

TEXT 4

Divine Servitude

Leviticus 25:55

כִּי לִי בְנֵי יִשְׂרָאֵל עֲבָדִים,
עֲבָדַי הֵם אֲשֶׁר הוֹצֵאתִי אוֹתָם מֵאֶרֶץ מִצְרָיִם.
אֲנִי ה׳ אֱלֹקֵיכֶם.

The Children of Israel belong to Me as servants.
They are My servants, whom I brought
out of Egypt. I am your G-d.

Watch the **Lubavitcher
Rebbe** address the
relationship between the
Exodus and receiving the
Torah, and what this can
teach us about freedom:
myjli.com/beyondright

TEXT 5

Only G-d's

Talmud, Bava Metzi'a 10a

BABYLONIAN TALMUD

A literary work of monumental proportions that draws upon the legal, spiritual, intellectual, ethical, and historical traditions of Judaism. The 37 tractates of the Babylonian Talmud contain the teachings of the Jewish sages from the period after the destruction of the 2nd Temple through the 5th century CE. It has served as the primary vehicle for the transmission of the Oral Law and the education of Jews over the centuries; it is the entry point for all subsequent legal, ethical, and theological Jewish scholarship.

כִּי לִי בְנֵי יִשְׂרָאֵל עֲבָדִים,

עֲבָדַי הֵם וְלֹא עֲבָדִים לַעֲבָדִים.

"The Children of Israel belong to Me as servants."
With this verse G-d is saying, "They are *My*
servants—not servants to other servants."

An illumination of the Passover *Haggadah* showing the Israelites working as slaves to Pharoah, interspersed with the text of the passages detailing the slavery. The first portion of this beautiful *Haggadah*, known as The Barcelona *Haggadah*, was copied in Spain in c. 1340. The second half, containing liturgy for Passover and Shavuot, was copied in France during the same time period. (British Library, London [Ad 14761])

TEXT 6

Jewish Nature

The Rebbe, Rabbi Menachem Mendel Schneerson,
Likutei Sichot 17, p. 75

**RABBI MENACHEM
MENDEL SCHNEERSON
1902–1994**

The towering Jewish
leader of the 20th
century, known as "the
Lubavitcher Rebbe," or
simply as "the Rebbe."
Born in southern
Ukraine, the Rebbe
escaped Nazi-occupied
Europe, arriving in
the U.S. in June 1941.
The Rebbe inspired
and guided the revival
of traditional Judaism
after the European
devastation, impacting
virtually every Jewish
community the world
over. The Rebbe often
emphasized that the
performance of just
one additional good
deed could usher in
the era of Mashiach.
The Rebbe's scholarly
talks and writings have
been printed in more
than 200 volumes.

אִיז דֶער "תַּעֲבְדוּן" נִיט אִין אַן אוֹפֶן וָואס בְּרֶעכְט דִי
מְצִיאוּת פוּן אַ אִידְן, נָאר אַדְרַבָּה:
דָאס גוּפָא אִיז דֶער עֶצֶם פוּן זַיין מְצִיאוּת . . .

אוּן וְוי חֲזַ״ל זָאגְן, "אֵין לְךָ בֶּן חוֹרִין אֶלָּא מִי שֶׁעוֹסֵק
בְּתַלְמוּד תּוֹרָה". דְלִכְאוֹרָה: תּוֹרָה אִיז דָאךְ אַן עִנְיָן
פוּן "תַּעֲבְדוּן", פוּן עַבְדוּת? וַויל דִי אֱמֶת'עַ טֶבַע
הַבְּרִיאָה פוּן אַ אִידְן אִיז צוּ טָאן תּוֹרָה וּמִצְווֹת, וּכְמַאֲמַר
הַמִשְׁנָה: "אֲנִי נִבְרֵאתִי לְשַׁמֵּשׁ אֶת קוֹנִי" . . .

דַוְוקָא וְוען עֶס אִיז דָא דֶער "תַּעֲבְדוּן",
אִיז עֶר אַן אֱמֶת'עֶר בֶּן חוֹרִין.

Service of G-d is not something that stifles the
identity of a Jew, G-d forbid. On the contrary, divine
service is the very core of every Jew's being. . . .

This is the meaning of the sages' teaching
that "no person is free except for those who
occupy themselves with Torah" (AVOT 6:2),
even though Torah observance is termed
"service." Observing Torah and *mitzvot* is the
true nature of a Jew, as the Mishnah teaches, "I
was created to serve my Creator." . . .

Only when serving G-d is a Jew truly free.

TEXT 7

Unnatural Control

Rabbi Tzadok Hakohen of Lublin, *Poked Akarim*, chapter 3

לִהְיוֹת בְּעַבְדוּת הוּא יְצִיאָה מִסֵּדֶר הַבְּרִיאָה. שֶׁבַּבְּרִיאָה נִמְסְרוּ רַק הַבַּעֲלֵי חַיִּים לְעַבְדוּת לְאָדָם וְשֶׁיִּרְדֶּה בָּהֶם, אֲבָל לֹא שֶׁיִּהְיֶה אָדָם עֶבֶד לְאָדָם.

Slavery is an unnatural state. The natural order of the universe is that animals are under the dominion of humans, but it is against the natural order for a human to be a slave to another human.

RABBI TZADOK HAKOHEN RABINOWITZ OF LUBLIN 1823–1900

Chasidic master and thinker. Rabbi Tzadok was born into a Lithuanian rabbinic family and later joined the Chasidic movement. He was a follower of the Chasidic leaders Rabbi Mordechai Yosef Leiner of Izbica and Rabbi Leibel Eiger. He succeeded Rabbi Eiger after his passing and became a rebbe in Lublin, Poland. He authored many works on Jewish law, Chasidism, kabbalah, and ethics, as well as scholarly essays on astronomy, geometry, and algebra.

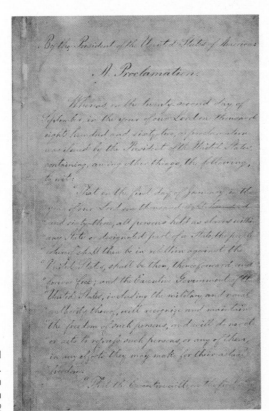

Handwritten and signed manuscript of U.S. President Abraham Lincoln's Emancipation Proclamation, 1862

II. DEBT RECOVERY

The Jewish perspective on the value of freedom has been clarified. It is left to be seen how this value is transported from the abstract and applied to the fine points of Jewish law. For this, we turn to the tomes that address financial shackles.

People need funds, borrow funds, and cannot always repay those funds. How does Jewish law handle individuals who fail to pay their debts? It was universally acceptable, for the majority of human history, for debtors to be imprisoned or forced into slavery for failure to repay. By contrast, Jewish law always insisted on a divergent approach to this issue.

CASE STUDY A   Rabbi Asher ben Yechiel, Responsa, *Kelal* 78:2

Reuben borrowed money from Shimon and failed to repay the loan. . . .

Reuben is now living with a relative, where he eats good food and dons expensive clothing. His wife is similarly expensively attired and even provides gifts to her friends. Reuben claims that all of this is provided by his relative, whereas he personally is penniless. He sits idle and refuses to engage in any labor or business of the type he always performed in the past because he knows that any money he earns will necessarily go toward repaying his loan.

RABBI ASHER BEN YECHIEL (ROSH) 1250–1328

Rabbi, author, and Talmudist, he is widely known by the acronym "Rosh." Rabbi Asher was a native of Germany, where he was a prominent disciple and successor of Rabbi Meir (Maharam) of Rothenburg. Due to the persecution and massacres of German Jewry under Emperor Rudolph I, Rabbi Asher was forced to flee, and in 1305, he arrived in Toledo, Spain. He is best known for his Halachic commentary on the Talmud. Rabbi Asher was the father of Rabbi Yaakov, the author of the *Arbaah Turim*.

You be the judge: What would be your decision if such a case came before you?

SHEPHERD
Yehoshua Wiseman, Israel. Jacob watches the sheep of Laban. As detailed in the Book of Genesis, Laban changed the terms of Jacob's wages as a shepherd 100 times so as to avoid paying Jacob what was rightfully due to him.

CASE STUDY B   Based on Britton v. Turner, 6 N.H. 481 (1834),
New Hampshire Superior Court

> Mr. Britton signed a contract to work for Mr.
> Turner for one year, for which he would be paid
> $120 in total—equaling $10 per month. But Britton
> ceased working after nine months, and Turner
> was only able to find a replacement worker for the
> remaining three months for $45—equaling $15
> per month. Turner did not pay Britton anything
> for his uncompleted contract, and Britton sued
> to collect pay for the work he performed.

How much do you think Mr. Britton should receive as payment for his work? Select the option closest to your view:

$0   Britton is in breach of contract. He has forfeited his right to any payment.

$90   Britton worked for 9 out of 12 months. He should be paid pro rata for 9 months.

$75   Britton would have been entitled to pro rata pay of $90, but his breach of contract forced Turner to hire a replacement at greater cost. Turner's loss from the affair totals $15, so this should be deducted from Britton's pay.

THERE'S MORE...

Note that Jewish law places restrictions on the length of some employment contracts; see Appendix (p. 129).

TEXT 8

Debt Recovery

Maimonides, *Mishneh Torah*,
Laws Pertaining to Lenders and Borrowers 2:1

דִּין תּוֹרָה שֶׁבִּזְמַן שֶׁיִּתְבַּע הַמַּלְוֶה אֶת חוֹבוֹ,
אִם נִמְצְאוּ לַלּוֹוֶה נְכָסִים מְסַדְּרִין לוֹ וְנוֹתְנִין
לְבַעַל חוֹבוֹ אֶת הַשְּׁאָר, כְּמוֹ שֶׁבֵּאַרְנוּ.

וְאִם לֹא נִמְצָא לַלּוֹוֶה כְּלוּם, אוֹ נִמְצְאוּ לוֹ דְּבָרִים
שֶׁמְּסַדְּרִין לוֹ בִּלְבַד, יֵלֵךְ הַלּוֹוֶה לְדַרְכּוֹ וְאֵין אוֹסְרִין אוֹתוֹ.

Scripture establishes that when creditors demand payment of debts, and the debtors own assets, the debtors' existential needs must first be provided for, following which the remainder of the debtors' assets are granted to the creditors.

If the debtors own no assets, or if their assets are only sufficient to provide for their existential needs, then nothing can be done to the debtors and they may not be imprisoned.

RABBI MOSHE BEN MAIMON (MAIMONIDES, RAMBAM) 1135–1204

Halachist, philosopher, author, and physician. Maimonides was born in Córdoba, Spain. After the conquest of Córdoba by the Almohads, he fled Spain and eventually settled in Cairo, Egypt. There, he became the leader of the Jewish community and served as court physician to the vizier of Egypt. He is most noted for authoring the *Mishneh Torah*, an encyclopedic arrangement of Jewish law; and for his philosophical work, *Guide for the Perplexed*. His rulings on Jewish law are integral to the formation of Halachic consensus.

Maimonides's handwritten signature authorizing a copy of his iconic work, the *Mishneh Torah*, dated to c. 1200. (Bodleian Library, Oxford, U.K. [MS. Hunt. 80])

Beyond Jurisdiction

Rabbi Asher ben Yechiel, Responsa, *Kelal* 78:2

וּמָה שֶׁטּוֹעֵן שִׁמְעוֹן שֶׁיַּעֲשֶׂה מְלָאכָה
כְּדֵי לִפְרֹעַ אֶת חוֹבוֹ, אֵין בֵּית דִּין כּוֹפִין אוֹתוֹ לְכָךְ . . . שֶׁלֹּא
יִשְׁלְחוּ בֵּית דִּין יָד בְּגוּפוֹ לְכוֹפוֹ לְהִשְׁתַּעְבֵּד וְלִפְרֹעַ חוֹבוֹ.

Shimon's request that Reuben work in order to
repay his debt is not something that the court can
compel. . . . The court cannot extend its jurisdiction
over Reuben's actual person by compelling him
to perform work in order to repay his debt.

An English debtors'
prison depicted in a copy
of Charles Dickens's
novel *The Pickwick
Papers*, illustrated by
Hablot Knight Browne
(1815–1882). (London:
Chapman and Hall, 1837)

TEXT 10

Prison Labor

Whitney Benns, "Prison Labor in America: How Is It Legal?"
The Atlantic, September 21, 2015

Once cleared by the prison doctor, [inmates] can be forced to work under threat of punishment as severe as solitary confinement. Legally, this labor may be totally uncompensated; more typically inmates are paid meagerly—as little as two cents per hour—for their full-time work in the fields, manufacturing warehouses, or kitchens. How is this legal? Didn't the Thirteenth Amendment abolish all forms of slavery and involuntary servitude in this country?

Not quite. In the shining promise of freedom that was the Thirteenth Amendment, a sharp exception was carved out. Section 1 of the Amendment provides: "Neither slavery nor involuntary servitude, except as punishment for crime whereof the party shall have been duly convicted, shall exist within the United States, or any place subject to their jurisdiction." Simply put: Incarcerated persons have no constitutional rights in this arena; they can be forced to work as punishment for their crimes.

TEXT 11

Debt Prison

Victorian Era England Debtor's Prisons History & Living Conditions, victorian-era.org

The debtors were sent to jail until they were able to pay off their debts. These were called debtor's prisons, a peculiar form of punishment. Indefinite incarceration was the mode of punishment. Sometimes, the convicts stayed with their families in the prison. Family members were free to come and go according to their wish. Therefore, even children were born and raised there.

The prisons were full of rats, lice and fleas. The prisoners were denied basic necessities of life such as food, water and clothing. It is said that these places were so dirty and filthy that around 25% of the inmates died due to these horrible living conditions.

The debtors were imprisoned and tortured at the pleasure of the creditors. When other countries of Europe had legislation limiting the debt imprisonment term to 1 year, England did not have such a law. When, in 1842, the Fleet Prison was closed, it was found that debtors were there for more than 30 years.

TEXT 12

Debtors' Freedom

Rabbi Yitzchak ben Sheshet, Responsa 484

RABBI YITZCHAK BEN SHESHET (RIVASH) 1326–1408

Halachist. Rivash studied under Rabbi Nisim of Gerona (Ran) in Barcelona and served as rabbi there and in other important Jewish communities in Spain. Because of the eruption of anti-Jewish riots in 1391, he fled to North Africa and settled in Algiers. He was the first to address the Halachic status of Marranos. Rivash's Halachic responsa are his most important work; they contain sources no longer extant and served, in part, as a basis for the Code of Jewish Law.

שְׁאֵלָה: רְאוּבֵן שֶׁלָּוָה מִשִּׁמְעוֹן, וְנִתְחַיֵּב לוֹ בְּקִנְיָן בְּכָל תֹּקֶף בִּתְפִישַׁת הַגּוּף . . . וְחֹק זֶה הוּא נָהוּג בְּמַלְכוּת אֲרָגוֹן שֶׁאִם אֵין לוֹ מִטַּלְטְלִין בְּנֵי חֹרִין שֶׁהוּא נִתְפָּשׂ בְּגוּפוֹ.

וְעַתָּה שִׁמְעוֹן הַמַּלְוֶה תָּבַע חוֹבוֹ מֵרְאוּבֵן הַלּוֶֹה וְנִמְצָא שֶׁאֵין לוֹ, בִּקֵּשׁ שֶׁיִּהְיֶה הַלּוֶֹה נִתְפָּשׂ בְּגוּפוֹ כְּפִי הַחִיּוּב שֶׁנִּתְחַיֵּב לוֹ.

וְהַלּוֶֹה טוֹעֵן שֶׁאֵינוֹ מִן הַדִּין שֶׁיִּהְיֶה נִתְפָּשׂ בְּגוּפוֹ, כִּי לֹא מָצִינוּ זֶה בְּדִין תּוֹרָה שֶׁיִּהְיֶה אָדָם מִיִּשְׂרָאֵל נִתְפָּשׂ בְּגוּפוֹ עַל שׁוּם שִׁעְבּוּד.

וְשָׁאַלְתָּ הַדִּין עִם מִי.

תְּשׁוּבָה: הַדִּין עִם רְאוּבֵן הַלּוֶֹה, שֶׁאֵין אָדָם יָכוֹל לְשַׁעְבֵּד עַצְמוֹ וּלְהַתְנוֹת לִהְיוֹת נִתְפָּשׂ בְּגוּפוֹ כִּדְאַמְרִינָן . . .

כְּתִיב כִּי לִי בְנֵי יִשְׂרָאֵל עֲבָדִים, וְלֹא עֲבָדִים לַעֲבָדִים . . . אֵין תְּנַאי מוֹעִיל לַעֲבוֹד בְּגוּפוֹ עַל כָּרְחוֹ אַף עַל פִּי שֶׁהוּא מְלֶאכֶת אוֹמָנָתוֹ הָרָגִיל בָּהּ. אֵין צָרִיךְ לוֹמַר שֶׁלֹּא יוֹעִיל תְּנַאי שֶׁיִּהְיֶה בְּמַסְגֵּר אָסוּר וּבְבֵית כֶּלֶא יוֹשְׁבֵי חֹשֶׁךְ.

Inquiry: Reuben borrowed money from Shimon. In the contract, Reuben put up his personal freedom as collateral. . . . For so is the law in Aragon: if a debtor does not own available assets from which his debt can be repaid, he is incarcerated.

Shimon the creditor now demands the repayment of his loan, but Reuben has no assets from which to pay. Shimon requests that Reuben be imprisoned, as he explicitly agreed to in advance.

Reuben argues that he cannot be imprisoned for his debt because there is no precedent in Jewish law for a person to be imprisoned due to a debt.

You requested my opinion on the law in such a case.

Response: Jewish law sides with Reuben the debtor. A person cannot consent to be incarcerated. . . .

The Torah states, "The Children of Israel belong to *Me* as servants," from which we derive that they cannot be made "servants to other servants." . . . No contract clause can allow for a person to be compelled to *work*, not even in his regular vocation. It goes without saying that no clause can allow for a person to be incarcerated and made to languish in a dark dungeon.

III. WORKERS' FREEDOM

The Jewish value of freedom does not only rule out forced labor, as clarified above. It also guides the nuances of the employer-employee relationship.

TEXT 13

The Right to Quit

Talmud, Bava Metzi'a 10a

פּוֹעֵל יָכוֹל לַחֲזֹר בּוֹ אֲפִלּוּ בַּחֲצִי הַיּוֹם . . .

דְּכְתִיב כִּי לִי בְנֵי יִשְׂרָאֵל עֲבָדִים (וַיִּקְרָא כה, נה).
עֲבָדַי הֵם, וְלֹא עֲבָדִים לַעֲבָדִים.

A worker has the right to withdraw from their employment even in the middle of the working day. . . .

This right emerges from the verse, "The Children of Israel belong to Me as servants" (LEVITICUS 25:55), whereby G-d is stating, "They are *My* servants—not servants to other servants."

TEXT 14

Payment for Partial Work

Rabbi Yaakov ben Asher, *Arbaah Turim, Choshen Mishpat* 333

**RABBI
YAAKOV BEN ASHER
(TUR, BAAL HATURIM)
C. 1269 – C. 1343**

Halachic authority and
codifier. Rabbi Yaakov
was born in Germany and
moved to Toledo, Spain,
with his father, the noted
Halachist Rabbi Asher,
to escape persecution.
He wrote *Arbaah Turim*
("*Tur*"), an ingeniously
organized and highly
influential code of Jewish
law. He is considered
one of the greatest
authorities on Halachah.

וְהַפּוֹעֵל, אִם הוּא שְׂכִיר יוֹם יָכוֹל לַחֲזֹר
אֲפִלּוּ בַּחֲצִי הַיּוֹם וְיָדוֹ עַל הָעֶלְיוֹנָה.

וְשָׁמִין כַּמָּה שָׁוֶה מַה שֶׁעָשָׂה וְנוֹטֵל, אֲפִלּוּ אִם נִתְיַקְּרָה
הַמְּלָאכָה שֶׁאֵינוֹ יָכוֹל לִגְוֹמְרָהּ בַּחֲצִי הַשָּׂכָר הַנִּשְׁאָר בְּיָדוֹ.

כְּגוֹן שֶׁשְׂכָרוֹ בְּח' דִּינָרִים לְיוֹם וְעָשָׂה עִמּוֹ חֲצִי הַיּוֹם, וַאֲפִלּוּ
אִם נִתְיַקְּרוּ שֶׁצָּרִיךְ לִתֵּן לְאַחֵר מֵחֲצִי הַיּוֹם הַנִּשְׁאָר ו' דִּינָרִין,
אֲפִלּוּ הָכִי צָרִיךְ לִתֵּן לָרִאשׁוֹן ד' דִּינָרִין מֵחֲצִי יוֹם שֶׁעָשָׂה.

וְלֹא אַמְרִינָן לֹא יִתֵּן לוֹ אֶלָּא ב' דִּינָרִין, כְּדֵי שֶׁתִּגָּמֵר
לוֹ מְלֶאכֶת הַיּוֹם בְּח' דִּינָרִין כְּפִי מָה שֶׁהִתְנָה.

An employee has the right to quit their job
even in the middle of the day and they are
given the upper hand when calculating
the pay they are entitled to receive.

The quitting employee is entitled to payment for
the value of work accomplished before quitting.
This remains true even if the market rate for
such work has since risen, leaving the employer
unable to hire another worker to complete
the job with the remainder of the funds.

For example: An employee was hired for eight
dinars per day, but quit halfway through the first
day. Even if the cost of this particular form of labor

has now risen to twelve dinars per day, so that a replacement worker for the second half of the day will charge six dinars, the quitting employee must still be paid four dinars for the half day of work.

We do not protect the employer from having to pay more than the eight dinars they originally intended to pay by deducting the expense of the replacement workers from the quitting worker's pay, which would leave the latter with only two dinars.

TEXT 15

Irreversible Loss

Rabbi Yaakov ben Asher, Ibid.

בְּדָבָר הָאָבֵד, כְּגוֹן שֶׁפִּשְׁתָּנוּ לַעֲלוֹת מִן הַמִּשְׁרָה
דְנִפְסָד אִם לֹא יַעֲלֶנּוּ, וְכָל כַּיּוֹצֵא בָּזֶה . . .

אִם הֵם אֲנוּסִים, כְּגוֹן שֶׁחָלָה אוֹ מֵת לוֹ מֵת, יְכוֹלִים לַחֲזוֹר
בָּהֶם וְיָדָם עַל הָעֶלְיוֹנָה לְשַׁלֵּם לָהֶם כָּל מָה שֶׁעָשׂוּ . . .

אֲבָל אִם אֵינָן אֲנוּסִים וְחָזְרוּ בָּהֶן,
יָדָן עַל הַתַּחְתּוֹנָה כֵּיוָן שֶׁהוּא דָּבָר אָבֵד.

If the work was time-sensitive and its neglect will cause irreversible damage, the quitting employee has the lower hand in the calculation of wages. For example, workers hired to remove flax from the water it was soaking in: if the flax is not punctually removed from the water, it will decay. . . .

If there are extenuating circumstances, such as illness or the death of a family member, the employee has the right to quit while retaining the upper hand in the calculation of their wages. . . .

Absent such circumstances, the employee is given the lower hand when calculating their pay because quitting prematurely may cause the employer an irreversible loss.

EXERCISE 4.2

Record a single word to describe the greatest benefit in working for *yourself*:

Record a single word to describe the greatest benefit in working for an *employer*:

Record a single word to describe the most significant drawback in working for *yourself*:

Record a single word to describe the most significant drawback in working for an *employer*:

TEXT 16

Employees vs. Contractors

Rashi, Bava Metzi'a 77a

RABBI
SHLOMO YITZCHAKI
(RASHI)
1040-1105

שֶׁאֲנִי לֵיה בֵּין שְׂכִירוּת לְקַבְּלָנוּת. גַּבֵּי שְׂכִירוּת אִיתָא לְהַאי טַעֲמָא דַעֲבָדַי הֵם וְלֹא עֲבָדִים לַעֲבָדִים, אֲבָל בְּקַבְּלָנוּת אֵין זֶה עֶבֶד אֶלָּא לְעַצְמוֹ.

The law granting an employee the right to quit does not extend to independent contractors. An employee is protected by the principle implied in the verse, "They are *My* servants—not servants to other servants," but this does not apply to independent contractors, for the contractors serve only themselves.

Most noted biblical and Talmudic commentator. Born in Troyes, France, Rashi studied in the famed *yeshivot* of Mainz and Worms. His commentaries on the Pentateuch and the Talmud, which focus on the straightforward meaning of the text, appear in virtually every edition of the Talmud and Bible.

SHTETL WATER CARRIER
Lionel Reiss (1894-1987),
pen and ink drawing, 1921

IV. ABSOLUTE FREEDOM

We now turn to applying the Jewish concept of freedom in our personal lives. Are we truly free? Are there any "slaveries" restricting us?

TEXT 17

Servants of Time

Rabbi Yehudah Halevi, *Diwan*, vol. 2, *Shirei Chol* 83

עַבְדֵי זְמָן עַבְדֵי עֲבָדִים הֵם;
עֶבֶד ה' הוּא לְבַד חָפְשִׁי.

עַל כֵּן בְּבַקֵשׁ כָּל אֱנוֹשׁ חֶלְקוֹ,
"חֶלְקִי ה'!" אָמְרָה נַפְשִׁי.

Servants of time are servants of servants;
A servant of G-d alone is free.

Therefore, when each person seeks their portion,
"My portion is G-d!" says my soul for me.

**RABBI YEHUDAH HALEVI
C. 1075–1141**

Noted author, physician, and poet. Rabbi Yehudah Halevi is best known as the author of the *Kuzari*, a philosophical work, written in the form of a discussion between a Jew, a Christian, and a Muslim before the King of the Khazars. In addition to the *Kuzari*, he wrote thousands of poems, of which only a few hundred survive today.

Are we subject to any form of slavery? **Rabbi Manis Friedman** discusses forms of "slavery" that are relevant to us:
myjli.com/beyondright

ALONE IN THE FOREST
Yehoshua Wiseman, Israel

QUESTION

What might it mean to be a servant of time?

EXERCISE 4.3

Can you identify any form of internal slavery that constrains you from realizing your purpose? How might you proceed in freeing yourself from such constraints?

KEY POINTS

1   Judaism teaches that true freedom is living the life we were created to live. This requires freedom from human masters, and devotion to G-d as the one true Master.

2   In the past, people could be forced into slavery for failing to repay debts. Even today, prisoners can legally be compelled to work. By contrast, Jewish law does not allow for anyone to be compelled to work against their will.

3   Debt prison was another once-ubiquitous tool for debt recovery. Jewish law has always banned debt prisons, even when stipulated in a loan agreement.

4   The employer-employee relationship requires an employee to surrender a certain degree of their freedom. Jewish law protects employees from veering too close to slavery by guaranteeing their right to quit mid-contract without penalty, unless doing so would cause the employer irretrievable loss.

APPENDIX

TEXT 18

Worker's Years

Isaiah 16:14

וְעַתָּה דִּבֶּר ה' לֵאמֹר, בְּשָׁלֹשׁ שָׁנִים כִּשְׁנֵי שָׂכִיר,
וְנִקְלָה כְּבוֹד מוֹאָב בְּכֹל הֶהָמוֹן הָרָב;
וּשְׁאָר מְעַט מִזְעָר, לוֹא כַבִּיר.

Now, G-d warns as follows: "In three years, like the years of a worker bound by contract, Mo'ab's glory will be publicly debased, leaving only a small remnant."

ISAIAH

Biblical book. The book of Isaiah contains the prophecies of Isaiah, who lived in the 7th–6th centuries BCE. Isaiah's prophecies contain stern rebukes for the personal failings of the contemporary people of Judea and the corruption of its government. The bulk of the prophecies, however, are stirring consolations and poetic visions of the future Redemption.

Miniature of the Israelites building a city as slaves to Pharoah in Egypt, decorating the page containing the passage "*Avadim hayinu*—We were slaves," in an Ashkenazi *Haggadah*, 15th century, Germany. (British Library, London [MS 14762])

TEXT 19

Term Limits

Rabbi Mordechai ben Hillel, Bava Metzi'a 459–460

כְּתִיב בִּישַׁעְיָה שָׁלֹשׁ שָׁנִים כִּימֵי שָׂכִיר . . .

מֶהַאי טַעֲמָא יֵשׁ לְזָהֵר לַמְלַמֵּד אוֹ לְסוֹפֵר אוֹ שְׁאָר מְלָאכוֹת
מִלְהַשְׂכִּיר עַצְמוֹ לִהְיוֹת בְּבֵית בַּעַל הַבַּיִת לִהְיוֹת בְּקֶבַע
עִמּוֹ . . . יוֹתֵר מִג' שָׁנִים. דְּכָל טְפֵי מִשָּׁלֹשׁ שָׁנִים נָפְקָא לֵיהּ
מִתּוֹרַת שָׂכִיר . . . קָא עָבַר עַל כִּי לִי בְנֵי יִשְׂרָאֵל עֲבָדִים.

The verse in Isaiah states, "In three years, like
the years of a worker bound by contract." . . .

Teachers, scribes, and other skilled workers should
not hire themselves out to live and work in their
employer's home for a period . . . longer than three
years. People bound by such a contract for more
than three years effectively lose their status as
a free worker . . . and transgress the verse, "The
Children of Israel belong to *Me* as servants."

**RABBI MORDECHAI
BEN HILLEL
C. 1240-1298**

Renowned codifier
and author, a devout
student of the Maharam
of Rothenburg. His
work, referred to as the
Mordechai, is a collection
of Tosafot, responsa,
quotes from various
other sages, and Halachic
decisions. This work
had a major influence
on talmudic scholarship
and is printed in the
back of most editions
of the Talmud. He was
martyred during a
massacre in Nuremburg,
Germany in 1298

Jewish Debt Collection Methods

Isaiah 16:14

Now, G-d warns as follows: "In three years, like the years of a worker bound by contract, Mo'ab's glory will be publicly debased, leaving only a small remnant."

Rabbi Yosef ben Shimon Kara (Mahari Kara), ad loc.

Workers commonly consent to employment contracts of up to three years. This is attested to in another Scriptural source as well—"He worked for you for six years, twice as long as a hired worker" (Deuteronomy 15:18). . . . The longest period for which a worker will sign a contract is three years.

Rabbi Mordechai ben Hillel, Bava Metzi'a 459–460

The verse in Isaiah states, "In three years, like the years of a worker bound by contract." . . .

Teachers, scribes, and other skilled workers should not hire themselves out to live and work in their employers' homes for a period longer than three years. People bound by contract for more than three years effectively lose their status as free workers . . . and transgress the verse, "The Children of Israel belong to Me as servants" (Leviticus 25:55).

Rabbi Yaakov Yeshayahu Blau, *Pitchei Choshen*, Laws of Employment 7:1

It is forbidden to enter into a work contract for more than three years of service. . . . However, this ban does not apply to those who are destitute to the point that they will be otherwise unable to obtain their basic necessities.

It also appears that this prohibition applies exclusively to workers who live permanently in their employers' residences for the duration of the agreed term of service, relying on their employers to provide all of their basic needs. For that arrangement, exclusively, appears similar to slavery.

By contrast, workers who provide several hours of work each day at their employers' residences before returning to their own homes are not subject to this restriction.

Debtors' Prisons

The problem of people failing to pay their debts has persisted since the genesis of lending.

The ancient world offered two primary responses: One was debt bondage, whereby debtors were compelled to perform labor to repay their debts. The alternative method was debtors' prisons, where debtors were held until they arranged the repayments of their debts or until others stepped up to the plate on their behalf.

This map indicates the dates of debt imprisonment abolishment in several major countries. For the purpose of this depiction, debt imprisonment is defined as the ability to imprison an individual for civil debts.

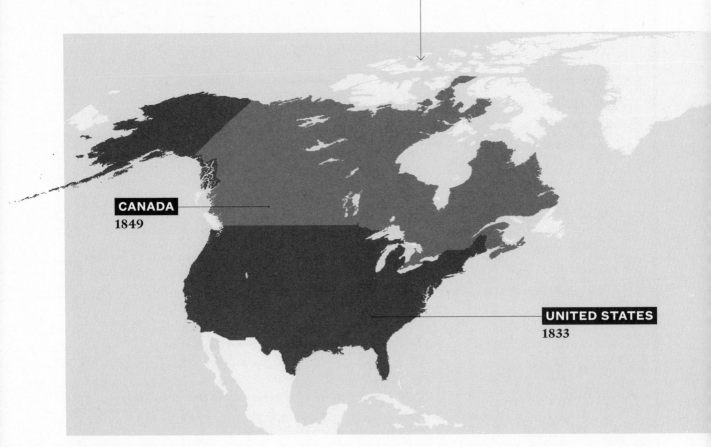

CANADA
1849

UNITED STATES
1833

Jewish Debt Collection Practices

The following excerpts of classic Jewish texts illustrate that Jewish law—since its origin at Mount Sinai—has consistently demanded that debtors be treated with dignity and respect. The practices of debt bondage and debt imprisonment were always prohibited.

ENGLAND
1869

GERMANY
1868

GREECE
2008

FRANCE
1867

EXODUS 22:24

When you lend money to My people, to the destitute individuals among you, do not act toward them like a creditor.

RASHI, AD LOC.

Do not present your claim against a debtor aggressively. If you are aware that the debtor lacks funds to repay the debt, do not act toward him as if you lent him money—rather, act as if you never lent him a penny. Do not embarrass your debtor.

DEUTERONOMY 24:10-13

When you extend a loan of any kind to your fellow, do not enter their home to obtain an object offered to you as collateral. Remain outside, and allow the individual to whom you are extending the loan to bring the collateral out to you.

If your fellow is poor, do not go to sleep [at night] with their collateral in your possession [if it serves a basic nocturnal utility]: Return the collateral by sunset so that they may sleep in their garment. Your fellow will bless you as a result, and G-d will regard it as a righteous act.

MAIMONIDES, *MISHNEH TORAH*, LAWS PERTAINING TO LENDERS AND BORROWERS 2:1

Scripture establishes that when creditors demand payment of debts, and the debtors own assets, the debtors' existential needs must first be provided for—following which, the remainder of the debtors' assets are granted to the creditors.

If the debtors own no assets, or if their assets are only sufficient to provide for their existential needs, then nothing can be done to the debtors and they may not be imprisoned.

We do not demand that debtors furnish proof of poverty, nor do we demand that they take an oath to declare that they have nothing with which to repay—as per the non-Jewish legal process. All of the above is included in the prohibition, "Do not act toward them like a creditor" (Exodus 22:24).

RABBI YOSEF CARO, SHULCHAN ARUCH, *CHOSHEN MISHPAT* 97:15

Debtors cannot be compelled to seek employment or perform any labor in order to pay their debts. Even if a debtor signed an explicit contract with his creditor stating that if he fails to repay his debt the creditor has permission to seize his person, this agreement is invalid and the debtor may not be imprisoned or compelled to work.

5

LESSON

A man holds on to the animal that he has acquired for the Passover sacrifice. Decoration from the Hijman Binger *Haggadah*, produced in 1796 by Chayim ben Mordechai Binger, whose illuminated manuscripts are housed in several collections worldwide. (Braginsky Collection 285)

BEYOND LAWFUL OWNERSHIP

Is the claim of ownership anything more than a subjective social agreement? A foundation of Chasidic thought is that material possessions contain spiritual energy that is specific to their owners. This perspective has legal and moral ramifications for how we relate to our possessions and the possessions of others.

I. OWNERSHIP THEORIES

The concept of ownership is the very foundation of civil law. In this lesson we explore the legal nature of ownership and learn how our definition of this can inform the way we use the possessions we own.

The following three Case Studies question our basic understanding of ownership.

CASE STUDY A

> David and Mark are friendly work colleagues. One day, David is terribly hungry at work and in a terrible rush, to boot. He notices that Mark had stored some food in the office refrigerator, but Mark is out of the office and unreachable. David reasons that since Mark is absent he does not need the food that day, and he could replace it for him tomorrow. Considering the circumstances and their general friendly relationship, David is certain Mark would allow him to eat his food.

In your opinion, may David eat Mark's food?

 Yes   No

CASE STUDY B

Sarah strolls along a street and discovers a bracelet lying on the sidewalk. She tries her hardest to track down its owner, to no avail.

In your opinion, may Sarah keep the bracelet?

◯ Yes ◯ No

CASE STUDY C

Leah strolls along the street and notices Naomi at a fair distance ahead of her. She watches in dismay as Naomi's bracelet falls into the gutter. Naomi tries unsuccessfully to extract the bracelet from the gutter. She throws her hands up in despair, gets into her car, and drives off. When Leah reaches that spot, she lifts the gutter cover and succeeds in extracting the bracelet.

In your opinion, may Leah (a) keep the bracelet, or (b) must she attempt to locate Naomi and return it?

◯ A ◯ B

Ownership as a Social Convention

Jeremy Waldron, "Property and Ownership," *The Stanford Encyclopedia of Philosophy* (Summer 2020 Edition), Edward N. Zalta (ed.)

Hobbes and Hume [argue] that there is no natural 'mine' or 'thine,' and that property must be understood as the creation of the sovereign state (Hobbes 1983 [1647]) or at the very least the artificial product of a convention "enter'd into by all the members of the society to bestow stability on the possession of . . . external goods, and leave every one in the peaceable enjoyment of what he may acquire by his fortune and industry" (Hume 1978 [1739], p. 489).

JEREMY WALDRON
1953–

Legal philosopher. A native of New Zealand, Jeremy Waldron received his doctorate in legal philosophy from Oxford University. Currently a professor of legal and political philosophy at NYU School of Law, Waldron has written extensively on the analysis and justification of private property and on the political and legal philosophy of John Locke.

Ownership as an Ontological Reality

Jeremy Waldron, Ibid.

John Locke (1988 [1689]), on the other hand, was adamant that property could have been instituted in a state of nature without any special conventions or political decisions. . . .

Locke did not base his resolution of this difficulty on any theory of universal (even tacit) consent. Instead, in the most famous passage of his

chapter on property, he gave a moral defense
of the legitimacy of unilateral appropriation.

> Though the Earth . . . be common to all
> Men, yet every Man has a Property in his
> own Person. This no Body has any Right to
> but himself. The Labour of his Body, and the
> Work of his Hands, we may say, are properly
> his. Whatsoever then he removes out of the
> State that Nature hath provided, and left it
> in, he hath mixed his Labour with, and joyned
> to it something that is his own, and thereby
> makes it his Property. It being by him removed
> from the common state Nature placed it in,
> it hath by this labour something annexed to
> it, that excludes the common right of other
> Men. (Locke 1988 [1689], II, para. 27)

QUESTION

**Of the two theories of ownership presented above
(Texts 1 and 2), which resonates more with you?**

● Text 1   ● Text 2

EXERCISE 5.1

Return to the opening Case Studies and respond to the questions based on the perspectives of Text 1 and Text 2.

	TEXT 1		TEXT 2	
CASE STUDY A **May David eat Mark's food?**	○ Yes	○ No	○ Yes	○ No
CASE STUDY B **May Sarah keep the bracelet?**	○ Yes	○ No	○ Yes	○ No
CASE STUDY C **May Leah (a) keep the bracelet, or (b) must she attempt to locate Naomi and return it?**	○ A	○ B	○ A	○ B

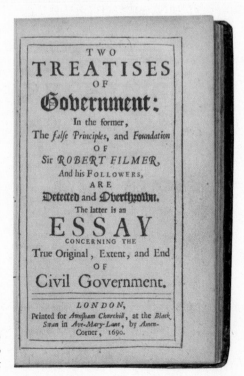

Title page from the 1690 edition of John Locke's *Two Treatises of Government*

II. A JEWISH THEORY OF OWNERSHIP

A key to unlocking the Jewish perspective on the meaning of owner-ship lies in a peculiar but fascinating biblical narrative concerning our forefather Jacob.

TEXT 3

A Mysterious Wrestling Bout

Genesis 32:24–25

וַיִּקָּחֵם וַיַּעֲבִרֵם אֶת הַנָּחַל וַיַּעֲבֵר אֶת אֲשֶׁר לוֹ. וַיִּוָּתֵר
יַעֲקֹב לְבַדּוֹ וַיֵּאָבֵק אִישׁ עִמּוֹ עַד עֲלוֹת הַשָּׁחַר.

Jacob took his family and transported them across the stream, and then he brought his possessions across. Jacob was left alone, and a man wrestled with him until the break of dawn.

JAKOB WORSTELT MET DE ENGEL—JACOB WRESTLES WITH THE ANGEL
Jan Luyken, etching on paper, Amsterdam, 1698 (Rijksmuseum [RP-P-OB-44.645])

TEXT 4

Your Money or Your Life?

Talmud, Chulin 91a

BABYLONIAN TALMUD

A literary work of
monumental proportions
that draws upon the legal,
spiritual, intellectual,
ethical, and historical
traditions of Judaism.
The 37 tractates of the
Babylonian Talmud
contain the teachings of
the Jewish sages from
the period after the
destruction of the 2nd
Temple through the 5th
century CE. It has served
as the primary vehicle
for the transmission
of the Oral Law and
the education of Jews
over the centuries; it
is the entry point for
all subsequent legal,
ethical, and theological
Jewish scholarship.

וַיִּוָּתֵר יַעֲקֹב לְבַדּוֹ, אָמַר רַבִּי אֶלְעָזָר, שֶׁנִּשְׁתַּיֵּר עַל פַּכִּין קְטַנִּים.

מִכָּאן לְצַדִּיקִים שֶׁחָבִיב עֲלֵיהֶם מָמוֹנָם יוֹתֵר מִגּוּפָם.

וְכָל כָּךְ לָמָּה, לְפִי שֶׁאֵין פּוֹשְׁטִין יְדֵיהֶן בְּגֶזֶל.

Rabbi Elazar explains that the reason Jacob
found himself alone and exposed to danger
was because he had returned to get some
small jars that had remained behind.

This episode informs us that righteous
individuals cherish their possessions more
than their own bodies. Why do they care so
much? For they never touch stolen property.

TEXT 5

The Soul of Ownership

Rabbi Yisrael Baal Shem Tov, *Keter Shem Tov* 218

הַתּוֹרָה חָסָה עַל מָמוֹנָם שֶׁל יִשְׂרָאֵל. וְלָמָּה כָּךְ, כִּי זֶה
כְּלָל גָּדוֹל שֶׁכָּל דָּבָר שֶׁאָדָם לוֹבֵשׁ אוֹ אוֹכֵל אוֹ מִשְׁתַּמֵּשׁ
בִּכְלִי, הוּא נֶהֱנֶה מֵהָרוּחָנִיּוּת שֶׁיֵּשׁ בְּאוֹתוֹ הַדָּבָר, כִּי
לוּלֵא אוֹתוֹ הָרוּחָנִיּוּת לֹא הָיָה שׁוּם קִיּוּם לְאוֹתוֹ דָּבָר.

וְיֵשׁ שָׁם נִיצוֹצִין קְדוֹשִׁים הַשַּׁיָּכִים לְשֹׁרֶשׁ נִשְׁמָתוֹ,
וּכְשֶׁהוּא מִשְׁתַּמֵּשׁ בְּאוֹתוֹ הַכְּלִי אוֹ אוֹכֵל מַאֲכָל אֲפִלּוּ

לְצֹרֶךְ גּוּפוֹ, הוּא מְתַקֵּן הַנִּצוֹצִין, כִּי אַחַר כָּךְ עוֹבֵד ה' בַּכֹּחַ
הַהוּא שֶׁבָּא לְגוּפוֹ מִלְּבוּשׁ אוֹ מַאֲכָל אוֹ שְׁאַר דְּבָרִים,
וּבְזֶה הַכֹּחַ עוֹבֵד לְהַשֵּׁם יִתְבָּרֵךְ, נִמְצָא מְתַקְּנָם . . .

לְכָךְ צָרִיךְ הָאָדָם לָחוּס עַל כֵּלָיו וְעַל כָּל דָּבָר
שֶׁיֵּשׁ לוֹ. דְּהַיְנוּ מִצַּד הַנִּצוֹצִין שֶׁיֵּשׁ בִּכְלִי זֶה,
בִּכְדֵי לָחוּס עַל הַנִּצוֹצִין הַקְּדוֹשִׁים.

**RABBI YISRAEL
BAAL SHEM TOV
(BESHT)
1698–1760**

Founder of the Chasidic
movement. Born in
Slutsk, Belarus, the
Baal Shem Tov was
orphaned as a child. He
served as a teacher's
assistant and clay digger
before founding the
Chasidic movement
and revolutionizing the
Jewish world with his
emphasis on prayer, joy,
and love for every Jew,
regardless of his or her
level of Torah knowledge.

The Torah is highly protective of people's
personal assets. This is a result of the major
spiritual principle that whichever material items
we use—the garments we wear, the food we
eat, or the utensils we utilize—we derive benefit
from the spiritual force present within each
item, for the existence of that item is sustained
by virtue of the spiritual presence within it.

Specific sparks of spirituality are embedded within
each item, and through divine providence, items
that are used by particular individuals harbor the
specific sparks that are related to their soul. As
a result, when we use a utensil, eat food, or wear
a garment—to satisfy our corporeal needs—we
thereby repair the spiritual sparks embedded within
them because we subsequently serve G-d with the
energy that our body acquired through that item. . . .

Watch an in-depth lecture
on ownership ethics in
Talmudic law:
myjli.com/beyondright

We must therefore be highly protective of our
possessions—of whatever we own—out of concern
for the individualized spiritual forces they possess.

III. TAKERS AND FINDERS

Naturally, the Jewish philosophy of ownership is reflected in practical Jewish law.

TEXT 6

Consumption and Assumptions

Rabbi Shneur Zalman of Liadi, *Shulchan Aruch HaRav*, *Choshen Mishpat*, Laws Pertaining to Lost Items and Deposits 4

RABBI SHNEUR ZALMAN OF LIADI (ALTER REBBE) 1745–1812

Chasidic rebbe, Halachic authority, and founder of the Chabad movement. The Alter Rebbe was born in Liozna, Belarus, and was among the principal students of the Magid of Mezeritch. His numerous works include the *Tanya*, an early classic containing the fundamentals of Chabad Chasidism; and *Shulchan Aruch HaRav*, an expanded and reworked code of Jewish law.

הַנִּכְנָס לַפַּרְדֵּס אוֹ לְגִנַּת חֲבֵרוֹ אָסוּר לוֹ לִלְקֹט פֵּרוֹת
שֶׁלֹּא מִדַּעַת הַבְּעָלִים, אַף עַל פִּי שֶׁבַּעַל הַפַּרְדֵּס
וְהַגִּנָּה הוּא אוֹהֲבוֹ וְרֵעוֹ אֲשֶׁר כְּנַפְשׁוֹ, וּבְוַדַּאי יִשְׂמַח
וְיָגִיל כְּשֶׁיֵּדַע לוֹ שֶׁנֶּהֱנָה זֶה מִפֵּרוֹתָיו. מִכָּל מָקוֹם,
כֵּיוָן שֶׁעַכְשָׁו אֵינוֹ יוֹדֵעַ מִזֶּה הֲרֵי הוּא נֶהֱנֶה בְּאִסּוּר.

וְכֵן כָּל כַּיּוֹצֵא בָּזֶה. וְצָרִיךְ לְהַזְהִיר לָרַבִּים
שֶׁנִּכְשָׁלִין בָּזֶה מֵחֲמַת חֶסְרוֹן יְדִיעָה.

If you enter a private orchard or garden, you may not pick its fruit without express permission from its owner.

This applies even if the owner of the orchard is your dear friend and will certainly be extremely pleased to hear that you enjoyed their fruits. Nevertheless, since the owner is unaware of your actions in real time, it is forbidden to benefit from the fruit.

Join a text-based Talmudic study of the mechanisms of transactions: **myjli.com/beyondright**

This principle applies in all similar cases. The public must be cautioned regarding this law, because it is commonly transgressed due to lack of awareness.

TEXT 7

Lost Property Law

"Lost Property," Cornell Law School Legal Information Institute, law.cornell.edu

At common law, a person who found lost personal property could keep it until and unless the original owner comes forward. This rule applied to people who discovered lost property in public areas, as well as to people who discovered lost property on their property.

Many jurisdictions have statutes that modify the common law's treatment of lost property. Typically, these statutes require lost personal property to be turned over to a government official, and that if the property is not claimed within a set period of time, it goes to the finder, and the original owner's rights to the property are terminated.

TEXT 8

Don't Ignore Lost Property

Deuteronomy 22:1–3

לֹא תִרְאֶה אֶת שׁוֹר אָחִיךָ אוֹ אֶת שֵׂיוֹ נִדָּחִים וְהִתְעַלַּמְתָּ
מֵהֶם. הָשֵׁב תְּשִׁיבֵם לְאָחִיךָ. וְאִם לֹא קָרוֹב אָחִיךָ
אֵלֶיךָ וְלֹא יְדַעְתּוֹ, וַאֲסַפְתּוֹ אֶל תּוֹךְ בֵּיתֶךָ וְהָיָה עִמְּךָ
עַד דְּרֹשׁ אָחִיךָ אֹתוֹ, וַהֲשֵׁבֹתוֹ לוֹ. וְכֵן תַּעֲשֶׂה לַחֲמֹרוֹ,
וְכֵן תַּעֲשֶׂה לְשִׂמְלָתוֹ, וְכֵן תַּעֲשֶׂה לְכָל אֲבֵדַת אָחִיךָ
אֲשֶׁר תֹּאבַד מִמֶּנּוּ וּמְצָאתָהּ, לֹא תוּכַל לְהִתְעַלֵּם.

If you see your fellow's ox or sheep straying, do not ignore it. Be sure to return it to its owner. If the owner is not near you, or if you do not know the owner's identity, take it home with you and keep it until they come for it, whereupon you shall return it. Do the same if you find their donkey, garment, or anything else they have lost. You may not ignore it.

EXERCISE 5.2

How does the biblical commandment of returning lost property in Text 8 differ from the secular legal position presented in Text 7?

1

2

3

TEXT 9

Perpetual Limbo

Maimonides, *Mishneh Torah*,
Laws of Stolen and Lost Property 13:10

**RABBI MOSHE
BEN MAIMON
(MAIMONIDES, RAMBAM)
1135-1204**

Halachist, philosopher,
author, and physician.
Maimonides was born
in Córdoba, Spain. After
the conquest of Córdoba
by the Almohads, he fled
Spain and eventually
settled in Cairo, Egypt.
There, he became the
leader of the Jewish
community and served
as court physician to
the vizier of Egypt.
He is most noted for
authoring the *Mishneh
Torah*, an encyclopedic
arrangement of
Jewish law; and for his
philosophical work,
Guide for the Perplexed.
His rulings on Jewish
law are integral to
the formation of
Halachic consensus.

הִכְרִיז אוֹ הוֹדִיעַ וְלֹא בָּאוּ הַבְּעָלִים, תִּהְיֶה
הַמְּצִיאָה מֻנַּחַת אֶצְלוֹ עַד שֶׁיָּבֹא אֵלִיָּהוּ.

If an announcement or notification regarding
the discovered item was made and the
owner did not come to claim it, the item
should remain in the possession of the finder
until the arrival of Elijah the Prophet.

TEXT 10A

Unmarked Finds

Maimonides, *Mishneh Torah*,
Laws of Stolen and Lost Property 14:1–2

וְלָמָּה פֵּרֵט הַשִּׂמְלָה, לִלְמֹד מִמֶּנָּה: מָה הַשִּׂמְלָה
מְיֻחֶדֶת שֶׁיֵּשׁ לָהּ סִימָנִין וְחֶזְקָתָהּ שֶׁיֵּשׁ לָהּ תּוֹבְעִין
וְחַיָּב לְהַחֲזִיר, אַף כָּל דָּבָר שֶׁיֵּשׁ לוֹ סִימָנִים הֲרֵי
הוּא בְּחֶזְקַת שֶׁיֵּשׁ לוֹ תּוֹבְעִין וְחַיָּב לְהַחֲזִיר.

אֲבָל דָּבָר שֶׁאֵין לוֹ תּוֹבְעִין, אֶלָּא נִתְיָאֲשׁוּ מִמֶּנּוּ הַבְּעָלִים,
הֲרֵי הוּא שֶׁל מוֹצְאוֹ אַף עַל פִּי שֶׁיֵּשׁ בּוֹ סִימָנִים.

**Rabbi Avrohom
Bergstein** explores the
Jewish laws of returning
lost objects and their
spiritual meaning:
myjli.com/beyondright

By mentioning the example of a garment
the Torah teaches us a law. Every garment
is unique and contains features by which

it can be identified. We therefore presume that its owner will seek its recovery, and we are obligated to return it. This establishes a principle: any article that has identifiable features is assumed to have an owner who seeks its recovery, and must therefore be returned.

By contrast, a lost article that no longer has owners who seek it—because they have despaired of its recovery—belongs to its finder, even if it bears identifying features.

HAGGADAH ELIYAHU HANAVI [PROPHET ELIJAH]
Zalman Kleinman, watercolor on paper, New York. Elijah the Prophet, who will answer all unresolved questions and conflicts that have arisen over the years of exile, traditionally comes to visit each home during the Passover *seder*. It is customary to open the door for him and read specific passages from the *Haggadah*.

TEXT 10B

Recovery from Despair

Maimonides, *Mishneh Torah*, Laws of Stolen and Lost Property 11:10

הַמּוֹצֵא אֲבֵדָה בְּזוּטוֹ שֶׁל יָם וּבִשְׁלוּלִיתוֹ שֶׁל נָהָר שֶׁאֵינוֹ
פּוֹסֵק, אַף עַל פִּי שֶׁיֵּשׁ בָּהּ סִימָן הֲרֵי זוֹ שֶׁל מוֹצְאָהּ

שֶׁנֶּאֱמַר, אֲשֶׁר תֹּאבַד מִמֶּנּוּ וּמְצָאתָהּ (דְּבָרִים כב, ג),
מִי שֶׁאֲבוּדָה מִמֶּנּוּ וּמְצוּיָה הִיא אֵצֶל. כָּל אָדָם יָצָאת זוֹ
שֶׁאֲבוּדָה מִמֶּנּוּ וּמִכָּל אָדָם, שֶׁזֶּה וַדַּאי שֶׁנִּתְיָאֵשׁ מִמֶּנָּה.

If you discover a lost item on the seashore, within reach of the tide, or in an area inundated by a flooding river, you may keep it. This applies even if the item has an identifying feature.

This law is derived from the command to return "an article that was lost to your fellow and you found it" (DEUTERONOMY 22:3), implying that the obligation extends to any circumstance in which an article is lost to its original owner but is likely to be found by others. This excludes an instance in which the item is assumed lost—not only to its owner but to all people. In such an instance, the owner certainly despairs of its recovery.

TEXT 11

Conscious Ownership

Rabbi Yehudah Loew of Prague, *Be'er Hagolah* 2:6

**RABBI YEHUDAH LOEW
(MAHARAL OF PRAGUE)
1525–1609**

Talmudist and
philosopher. Maharal
rose to prominence
as leader of the famed
Jewish community
of Prague. He is the
author of more than a
dozen works of original
philosophic thought,
including *Tiferet Yisrael*
and *Netzach Yisrael*. He
also authored *Gur Aryeh,*
a supercommentary
to Rashi's biblical
commentary; and a
commentary on the
nonlegal passages of
the Talmud. He is
buried in the Old Jewish
Cemetery of Prague.

וּמִפְּנֵי שֶׁהַמָּמוֹן שֶׁל אָדָם אֵינוֹ עֶצֶם מֵעַצְמוֹ וּבְשָׂר
מִבְּשָׂרוֹ, רַק הוּא קִנְיָנוֹ אֲשֶׁר הוּא שַׁיָּךְ לָאָדָם.

וּלְפִיכָךְ כַּאֲשֶׁר נֶאֱבַד הַמָּמוֹן מִמֶּנּוּ, שֶׁאֵין הַמָּמוֹן בִּרְשׁוּתוֹ,
כִּי כָּל אֲבֵדָה הַמָּמוֹן יוֹצֵא מִתַּחַת רְשׁוּתוֹ, הֲרֵי הַמָּמוֹן
עַצְמוֹ אֵינוֹ בִּרְשׁוּתוֹ, וְגַם דַּעְתּוֹ אֵין עָלָיו, שֶׁנִּתְיָאֵשׁ וְהוֹצִיא
אֶת הַמָּמוֹן מִלִּבּוֹ, הֲרֵי דָּבָר זֶה אֵינוֹ עוֹד מָמוֹנוֹ כְּלָל,
שֶׁאֵינוֹ בִּרְשׁוּתוֹ, וְגַם אֵינוֹ בְּדַעְתּוֹ, וְהוּא הֶפְקֵר גָּמוּר.

Your property is not a part of your body from
which you cannot be separated. Rather, it is your
possession—something external that belongs to you.

Therefore, if you lose an item and it is no longer
in your possession—and you have also removed it
from your consciousness through abandoning the
hope of its recovery—strict principles of ownership
dictate that it is no longer yours. It is ownerless.

TEXT 12

Beyond the Letter of the Law

Rabbi Shneur Zalman of Liadi, *Shulchan Aruch HaRav*, *Choshen Mishpat*, Laws Pertaining to Lost Items and Deposits 18

וְכָל זֶה מִשּׁוּרַת הַדִּין. אֲבָל טוֹב וְיָשָׁר לַעֲשׂוֹת לִפְנִים מִשּׁוּרַת הַדִּין . . . אַף עַל פִּי שֶׁכְּבָר נִתְיָאֲשׁוּ.

All the above accords with the letter of the law. Nevertheless, the good and proper course of action is to extend yourself beyond the letter of the law . . . and return a lost item even if its owner already despaired of its recovery.

TEXT 13

Standing on Principle

Rabbi Yehudah Loew of Prague, *Be'er Hagolah* 2:6

בְּפֶרֶק ב' דְּבָבָא מְצִיעָא (כא, א) אָמְרוּ שָׁם שֶׁאֵין צָרִיךְ לְהַחֲזִיר הָאֲבֵדָה אַחַר יֵאוּשׁ בְּעָלִים. וְדָבָר זֶה נִרְאֶה לִבְנֵי אָדָם רָחוֹק, שֶׁיִּקַּח אָדָם אֶת שֶׁאֵינוֹ שֶׁלּוֹ, וְהוּא לֹא עָמַל וְלֹא טָרַח, וְיַחְמֹד מָמוֹן אַחֵר.

וְדָבָר זֶה אֵינוֹ לְפִי דַת הַנִּימוּסִית, כִּי דַת הַנִּימוּסִית מְחַיֵּב לְהַחֲזִיר הָאֲבֵדָה אַף אַחַר יֵאוּשׁ בַּעַל הָאֲבֵדָה מִן הָאֲבֵדָה. וְסִבָּה זֹאת, כִּי דַת הַנִּימוּסִית מְחַיֵּב דָּבָר מָה שֶׁרָאוּי לַעֲשׂוֹת לְפִי תִּקּוּן הָעוֹלָם, אַף כִּי אֵין הַשֵּׂכֶל מְחַיֵּב דָּבָר הַהוּא, רַק שֶׁכָּךְ הוּא תִּקּוּן הָעוֹלָם . . .

וְכֵן לְהֵפֶךְ: אִם מָצָא כְּלֵי כֶסֶף וּכְלֵי זָהָב, וְהִכְרִיז עָלָיו
פַּעַם אַחַת וּשְׁתַּיִם, וְלֹא דָרַשׁ אָדָם אַחַר הָאֲבֵדָה בְּשָׁנָה
אוֹ שְׁנָתַיִם, הֲרֵי הוּא מְעַכֵּב לְעַצְמוֹ וּמִשְׁתַּמֵּשׁ בַּכְּלֵי
הַהוּא. כִּי אֵין בָּזֶה תִּקּוּן עוֹלָם, אַחַר שֶׁהִכְרִיז עָלָיו כַּמָּה
פְּעָמִים וְהִמְתִּין שָׁנָה אוֹ שְׁנָתַיִם אוֹ יוֹתֵר, שׁוּב לֹא יָבוֹא.

וְדָבָר זֶה אֵינוֹ לְפִי הַתּוֹרָה, כִּי אִם מָצָא כְּלֵי כֶסֶף אוֹ כְּלֵי זָהָב,
וְהִכְרִיז עָלָיו פְּעָמִים הַרְבֵּה, אֲסוּרִים לוֹ לְעוֹלָם, רַק יְהֵא מֻנָּח
עַד שֶׁיָּבֹא אֵלִיָּהוּ, לֹא יִגַּע בָּהֶם לְעוֹלָם. הֲרֵי שֶׁהֶחֱמִירוּ מְאֹד.

וְכָל זֶה, כִּי דִּבְרֵי חֲכָמִים עַל פִּי הַתּוֹרָה, שֶׁכָּל
דִּבְרֵי תוֹרָה מְשֹׁעָרִים בְּשֵׂכֶל. וְכַאֲשֶׁר כָּרָאוּי
לְפִי הַשֵּׂכֶל, כָּךְ רָאוּי לַעֲשׂוֹת . . .

וְאִם יֹאמַר הָאָדָם, דְּסוֹף סוֹף יֵשׁ לְהַחֲזִיר הָאֲבֵדָה
מִצַּד הָרָאוּי, כְּדֵי שֶׁלֹּא יַגִּיעַ הֶזֵּק לַחֲבֵרוֹ.

הֲלֹא דָבָר זֶה אָמְרוּ שֶׁיֵּשׁ לְהַחֲזִיר הָאֲבֵדָה, אַף אַחַר
יֵאוּשׁ בַּעַל הָאֲבֵדָה. לֹא מִצַּד הַחִיּוּב, כִּי מִצַּד הַחִיּוּב
אֵין צָרִיךְ, כְּמוֹ שֶׁהִתְבָּאֵר, רַק מִצַּד הַחֶסֶד. וְהוֹצִיאוּ
הַדָּבָר הַזֶּה (בָּבָא מְצִיעָא ל, ב) מִן הַכָּתוּב . . . שֶׁיֵּשׁ
לָאָדָם לַעֲשׂוֹת לִפְנִים מִשּׁוּרַת הַדִּין וְלֹא יַעֲמִיד אֶת
דְּבָרָיו עַל הַדִּין, וְזֶה מִצַּד שֶׁרָאוּי לַעֲשׂוֹת חֶסֶד.

וּבָזֶה הַתּוֹרָה שְׁלֵמָה בְּתַכְלִית הַשְּׁלֵמוּת, שֶׁהִיא תּוֹרַת
אֱמֶת מָה שֶׁהוּא מְחַיֵּב לְפִי הַשֵּׂכֶל, וְגַם לִמְּדָה הַתּוֹרָה
לַעֲשׂוֹת הַטּוֹב וְהַחֶסֶד מָה שֶׁרָאוּי לַעֲשׂוֹת מִצַּד הַחֶסֶד,
עַד שֶׁלֹּא תֶחְסַר כֹּל בָּהּ. וְעִם הַתּוֹרָה הָאֱמֶת וְהַשָּׁלוֹם.

Our sages state that we are not required to return a lost object to its original owner once the owner has despaired of its recovery (TALMUD, BAVA METZI'A 21A). This seems unfair to many people's sensibilities. How can we appropriate someone else's belongings for which we neither toiled nor troubled?

However, the Torah's legal system is not a system of pragmatic ethical conventions. In a pragmatic ethical system, it would make sense to return a lost object even if the owner despaired of recovering it because such systems are designed to maintain social order, and for the sake of social order it seems more plausible to grant the lost object to the original owner. . . .

Conversely, pragmatic ethical conventions dictate that if we find gold or silver vessels with identifying features and publicize our find once or twice, then if the owner fails to come forward to claim them within a year or two, we may keep them for our own use. After all, considerable time has elapsed, and despite our diligence in publicizing the find, the owner has not stepped forward. Apparently, the owner will never appear, and therefore keeping the items will not rattle the social order.

But in Torah law this would not be the case. Even if we publicized the lost property numerous times, we may never claim it as our own. It must be stored safely "until the arrival of Elijah the Prophet."

Torah law takes this extremely stringent stance because it is based on strict logical principles free of pragmatic reasoning. . . .

Some might object: True, strict principles of ownership dictate that despair of an object should result in the automatic suspension of ownership. But from an ethical standpoint, shouldn't one return the object anyway in order to spare its owner from suffering a loss?

The answer is that our sages indeed assumed that position: They stated that we *should* return the item even after its owner has lost all hope of its recovery—not as a legal obligation, but as an act of kindness. The sages derived this, too, from the Torah, . . . which calls upon us to step beyond the strict letter of the law and act kindly to others (TALMUD, BAVA METZI'A 30B).

In this way the Torah is a perfect system. It maintains laws that are consistent with true principles of logic, and at the same time it teaches us to act with kindness.

IV. SOULFUL OWNERSHIP

Having clarified the Jewish theory of ownership and its practical ramifications on specific legal questions, our final step is to explore what this theory of ownership can teach us about how to use our property and how to relate to the property of others.

EXERCISE 5.3

Compare John Locke's theory of ontological ownership, presented in Text 2, with Rabbi Yisrael Baal Shem Tov's theory of ontological ownership presented in Text 5.

How do these theories of ownership differ?

What are the ramifications of these distinctions?

Fruits of Battle

Deuteronomy 20:19

כִּי תָצוּר אֶל עִיר יָמִים רַבִּים לְהִלָּחֵם עָלֶיהָ
לְתָפְשָׂהּ, לֹא תַשְׁחִית אֶת עֵצָהּ.

When you lay siege to a city for an extended
period of time as part of a battle to capture
it, do not destroy its [fruit-bearing] trees.

Do Not Destroy

Maimonides, *Mishneh Torah*, Laws of Kings and Wars 6:10

וְלֹא הָאִילָנוֹת בִּלְבַד. אֶלָּא כָּל הַמְשַׁבֵּר כֵּלִים,
וְקוֹרֵעַ בְּגָדִים, וְהוֹרֵס בִּנְיָן, וְסוֹתֵם מַעְיָן, וּמְאַבֵּד
מַאֲכָלוֹת דֶּרֶךְ הַשְׁחָתָה, עוֹבֵר בְּלֹא תַשְׁחִית.

This prohibition is not restricted to fruit trees.
Anyone that shatters utensils, tears garments,
destroys buildings, plugs a natural spring, or ruins
food—with destructive intent—transgresses
the Torah's prohibition of "do not destroy."

EXERCISE 5.4

How might I apply to my personal life the idea of soulful ownership?

Only a few complete copies of the famous Prague *Haggadah*, completed on December 30, 1526, remain today. Printed in Prague, one of the first cities to print Hebrew books, by brothers Gershom and Grunim Katz, the *Haggadah* contains many woodcut illustrations and decorative borders. Here a man searches his home for *chametz*, leavened products that are forbidden to be owned or consumed on Passover, a pre-Passover custom that is followed by a declaration of forgoing ownership of any *chametz* that might have been overlooked. (Braginsky Collection 211)

KEY POINTS

1 Jewish mysticism teaches us that ownership
reflects a spiritual relationship between the
owner and the possessions. Our belongings hold
a spiritual energy that only we can harness.

2 The Jewish theory of soul-related ownership
does not just provide a definition of ownership.
It also informs our *use* of our property and our
manner of relating to the property of others.

3 Jewish ownership laws are based on strict
principles. As a result, Jewish law does not
allow us to take someone else's property
without advance permission, even if we're
certain the owner would approve.

4 Jewish law is very stringent regarding the
return of lost property, obligating us to
proactively retrieve lost items and seek out
the owner. This obligation has no end date.

5 The strict principles of Jewish law sometimes
result in leniency as well, such as allowing
us to keep a found item if circumstances

make it clear that the original owner has despaired of its recovery. Nevertheless, we are encouraged to step beyond the strict letter of the law and return the item.

Perspectives on Ownership

WILLIAM BLACKSTONE 1723–1780

📖 *Commentaries on the Laws of England, vol. 2, ch. 1*

But when mankind increased in number, craft, and ambition, it became necessary to entertain conceptions of more permanent dominion; and to appropriate to individuals not the immediate use only, but the very substance of the thing to be used. Otherwise innumerable tumults must have arisen, and the good order of the world be continually broken and disturbed, while a variety of persons were striving who should get the first occupation of the same thing, or disputing which of them had actually gained it.

JEREMY BENTHAM 1748–1832

📖 *Principles of the Civil Code, Part 1: "Objects of the Civil Law"*

Property is only a foundation of expectation—the expectation of deriving certain advantages from the thing said to be possessed, in consequence of the relations in which one already stands to it.

There is no form, or colour, or visible trace, by which it is possible to express the relation which constitutes property. It belongs not to physics, but to metaphysics: it is altogether a creature of the mind....

The idea of property consists in an established expectation—in the persuasion of power to derive certain advantages from the object, according to the nature of the case.

But this expectation, this persuasion, can only be the work of the law. I can reckon upon the enjoyment of that which I regard as my own, only according to the promise of the law, which guarantees it to me. It is the law alone which allows me to forget my natural weakness: it is from the law alone that I can enclose a field and give myself to its cultivation, in the distant hope of the harvest.

JOHN LOCKE 1632–1704

📖 *Second Treatise of Civil Government, Chapter V, "Of Property"*

I shall endeavor to show, how men might come to have a property in several parts of that which G-d gave to mankind in common, and that without any express compact of all the commoners....

Though the Earth, and all inferior Creatures be common to all Men, yet every Man has a Property in his own Person. This no Body has any Right to but himself. The Labour of his Body, and the Work of his Hands, we may say, are properly his. Whatsoever then he removes out of the State that Nature hath provided, and left it in, he hath mixed his Labour with, and joyned to it something that is his own, and thereby makes it his Property. It being by him removed from the common state Nature placed it in, hath by this labour something annexed to it, that excludes the common right of other Men. For this Labour being the unquestionable Property of the Labourer, no man but he can have a right to what that is once joyned to, at least where there is enough, and as good left in common for others.

Forty days before an embryo takes form, a proclamation is issued by Heaven regarding its future, "The daughter of so-and-so is destined to marry so-and-so; such and such a house is destined to be inhabited by so-and-so; such and such a field is destined to be farmed by so-and-so."

RABBI TZADOK OF LUBLIN 1823–1900

🏛 *Tzidkat Hatzadik* 86

Whatever we own—our home, livestock, financial assets, and all else—is linked to the root of our souls.

For all inanimate objects, plant life, and animals are linked to human souls and derive their life force from particular human souls. The specific property that we own is comprised of the very assets and items that derive their sustenance from our souls.

🏛 *Peri Tzadik*, Pesach, p. 36b

Our sages taught that "righteous individuals cherish their possessions more than their own persons because they never touch stolen property" (Talmud, Sotah 12a). This informs us that the righteous take only from what G-d has entrusted to them. This is the significance of the phrase,

"My allotted bread" (Proverbs 30:8), referring to the portion allotted to an individual by G-d.

Anything other than one's allotted portion is referred to as stolen—"As if it were stolen from G-d and the Jewish people" (Talmud, Berachot 36b)—because the entire world belongs to G-d, and whatever was not created for a specific individual is considered by those who are righteous as akin to stolen property; they will not touch it.

Therefore, the righteous deeply cherish the money or assets that were designated for them, and, indeed, were created specifically for their use—to the extent that our forefather Jacob risked his life to retrieve such possessions.

Our holy teacher, Rabbi Mordechai Yosef Leiner of Izbica, taught in the name of his teacher, Rabbi Simcha Bunim of Peshischa, who received this teaching from the saintly Rabbi Yaakov Yitzchak (the "Yid Hakadosh"): righteous individuals must utilize each material possession with which they are associated, even if it demands self-sacrifice.

Our forefather Jacob recognized that the small jars he had left behind were his property and therefore related to his soul and created for his use. This awareness prompted him to risk his life for the sake of retrieving them.

The Mitzvah of "Do Not Destroy"

Deuteronomy 20:19

When you lay siege to a city for an extended period of time as part of a battle to capture it, do not destroy its fruit-bearing trees.

▼

SCOPE

Maimonides, *Mishneh Torah*, Laws of Kings and Wars 6:10

This prohibition is not restricted to fruit trees. Anyone that shatters utensils, tears garments, destroys buildings, plugs a natural spring, or ruins food—with destructive intent—transgresses the Torah's prohibition of "do not destroy."

Maimonides, *Mishneh Torah*, Laws of Mourning 14:24

The Torah instructs us not to destroy property and throw useful entities to waste. It is better to donate such items to the needy rather than to throw them to maggots and worms.

Rabbi Yonah of Gerona, *Shaarei Teshuvah* 3:82

This prohibition also cautions us against wasting money, even the minutest sum.

▼

REASON

Sefer Hachinuch, Mitzvah 529

The reason for this negative commandment is self-obvious—it trains us to cherish goodness and productivity. . . . This is the path of the pious and the righteous: they love peace, rejoice in the good of others and draw others closer to the Torah, and they will not destroy even a single grain of mustard seed.

▼

EXCEPTIONS

Talmud, Shabbat 129a

After Shmuel underwent bloodletting, they chopped a teak wood chair into pieces for him to build a fire to warm himself. Similarly, when Rav Yehudah underwent this procedure, they broke an ebony wood table to use as firewood, and for Rabah a bench was used.

Abaye challenged Rabah: "In breaking the furniture, did you not violate the prohibition of 'do not destroy'?" Rabah responded, "The prohibition of 'do not destroy' with respect to my own body is more important to me!"

Talmud, Shabbat 140b

Rav Chisda stated, "One who is able to eat barley bread but instead eats wheat bread [despite its higher price] violates the prohibition of 'do not destroy.'" Similarly, Rav Papa stated, "One who is able to drink beer but instead drinks wine [at greater cost] violates the prohibition of 'do not destroy.'"

However, the above statements notwithstanding, there is no actual problem in doing so because the prohibition of "do not destroy" with regard to one's own body

is of greater consideration. [An improvement of health through higher-quality food takes precedence over the conservation of funds.]

SUMMARY

Rabbi Shneur Zalman of Liadi, *Shulchan Aruch Harav,*
Choshen Mishpat, **Laws Pertaining to Protection of Life**

Just as we are instructed to exercise caution to avoid harm or damage to our bodies, so are we instructed to avoid ruining or destroying our possessions. Whoever breaks utensils, tears clothing, destroys a building, blocks a stream, ruins food or drink, throws money away, or damages anything that is suitable for human benefit transgresses the negative commandment contained in the verse, "Do not destroy." . . . .

The above applies only if we act with destructive intent. Conversely, we are allowed to destroy an entity to derive benefit provided that there is no alternative method of obtaining that benefit. For example, we may remove a fruit tree that is damaging the soil or harming other trees that are more valuable than the problematic tree. Similarly, if we require the ground on which the tree is growing for construction, or if

the tree blocks our window, it may be cut. If the tree is more valuable for use as wood for construction than for its fruit, it may also be removed. The same principle applies to all similar considerations.

Needless to state, it is certainly permissible to damage an item to provide direct personal benefit. For example, we may burn a chair or table to provide heat if we lack alternative wood.

BEYOND PRESUMPTION OF INNOCENCE

*While a presumption of innocence can protect
defendants from liability, it is not quite a declaration
of uprightness. Jewish law goes so far as to presume
every person's core goodness. In this class we explore
the sources of this positive perspective on human
nature and its practical ramifications.*

I. POSITIVE BIAS

This chapter delves into the internal courts of interpersonal appraisals that operate relentlessly in all hearts and minds—to examine the value of judging others favorably. It is first necessary to clarify the psychological as well as philosophical roots of this value, for the sake of determining the unique manner in which such favorable appraisals guide the Jewish legal system.

The following exercises and texts probe our personal biases and our treatment of them.

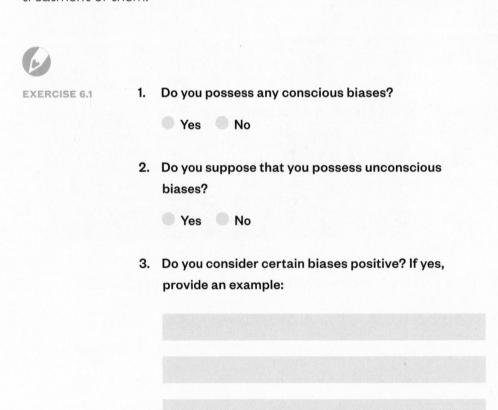

EXERCISE 6.1

1. **Do you possess any conscious biases?**

    ⬤ Yes ⬤ No

2. **Do you suppose that you possess unconscious biases?**

    ⬤ Yes ⬤ No

3. **Do you consider certain biases positive? If yes, provide an example:**

TEXT 1A

Prejudicial Bias

Oxford Online English Dictionary (Lexico), "bias"

Prejudice in favor of or against one thing, person, or group compared with another, usually in a way considered to be unfair.

TEXT 1B

Temperamental Inclination

Merriam-Webster.com Dictionary, "bias"

An inclination of temperament or outlook.

Especially: a personal and sometimes unreasoned judgment.

QUESTION

How do these definitions of bias differ?

EXERCISE 6.2

The following chart lists four fairly common personal lapses/negative occurrences. It asks us how we interpret them when they happen to us, and how we interpret them when they happen to others.

Fill in the chart with your own interpretations, or select some of the options provided below the chart.

	ME	OTHERS
CAME HOME LATE		
BAD MOOD		
MISSED APPOINTMENT		
LEFT A MESS		

Irresponsible	Difficult person
Slob	Overwhelmed
Bad day	Unexpected traffic
Something came up	Disorganized

TEXT 2A

Righteous Judgment

Leviticus 19:15

בְּצֶדֶק תִּשְׁפֹּט עֲמִיתֶךָ.

You shall judge your fellow with righteousness.

TEXT 2B

Giving a Positive Spin

Sefer Hachinuch, Mitzvah 235

וְעוֹד יֵשׁ בִּכְלַל מִצְוָה זוֹ, שֶׁרָאוּי לְכָל אָדָם לָדוּן אֶת חֲבֵרוֹ
לְכַף זְכוּת, וְלֹא יְפָרֵשׁ מַעֲשָׂיו וּדְבָרָיו אֶלָּא לְטוֹב . . .

בְּמָה שֶׁאָמַרְנוּ שֶׁכָּל אָדָם חַיָּב לָדוּן חֲבֵרוֹ לְכַף זְכוּת,
שֶׁהוּא בִּכְלַל הַמִּצְוָה, יִהְיֶה סִבָּה לִהְיוֹת בֵּין אֲנָשִׁים
שָׁלוֹם וְרֵעוּת . . . עִם סִלּוּק הַחֲשָׁד אִישׁ בְּאִישׁ.

Included in this commandment is the instruction to each individual to judge their fellows favorably and to deliberately interpret their conduct and statements in a positive light. . . .

Through judging others favorably we will foster peace and harmony among people . . . as a result of eliminating mutual suspicion.

SEFER HACHINUCH

A work on the biblical commandments. Four aspects of every mitzvah are discussed in this work: the definition of the mitzvah; ethical lessons that can be deduced from the mitzvah; basic laws pertaining to the observance of the mitzvah; and who is obligated to perform the mitzvah, and when. The work was composed in the 13th century by an anonymous author who refers to himself as "the Levite of Barcelona." It has been widely thought that this referred to Rabbi Aharon Halevi of Barcelona (Re'ah); however, this view has been contested.

For more about judging others favorably, watch: **myjli.com/beyondright**

II. HUMAN NATURE

Text 2B asserts that striving to view others with the same positive bias we afford ourselves generates a happier and more peaceful society. Granted, such a perspective can be beneficial—but is it accurate, or is it a form of illusionary living?

TEXT 3

Man Is a Wolf to Man

Sigmund Freud, *Civilization and Its Discontents*, trans. James Strachey (New York: W. W. Norton and Co., 2005), pp. 103–104

**SIGMUND FREUD, PHD
1856–1939**

Neurologist and founder of psychoanalysis. Freud may justly be called the most influential intellectual legislator of his age. His creation of psychoanalysis was at once a theory of the human psyche, a therapy for the relief of its ills, and an optic for the interpretation of culture and society. Despite repeated criticisms, attempted refutations, and qualifications of Freud's work, its spell remained powerful well after his death and in fields far removed from psychology.

Men are not gentle creatures who want to be loved, and who at the most can defend themselves if they are attacked; they are, on the contrary, creatures among whose instinctual endowments is to be reckoned a powerful share of aggressiveness. . . . *Homo homini lupus* ["Man is a wolf to man"]. Who, in the face of all his experience of life and of history, will have the courage to dispute this assertion?

PULL
Sarah Stone.
Inner conflict and vying inclinations are built into human nature.

A Positive View of Human Nature

Carl Rogers, *On Becoming a Person: A Therapist's View of Psychotherapy* (London: Constable, 1974), pp. 70–71

CARL ROGERS
1902–1987

Psychologist. Born in Chicago, Carl Rogers received his PhD in clinical psychology from Columbia University. Rogers taught psychology at various American universities and established the Center for Studies of the Person. Considered one of the most influential psychologists of all time, Rogers advocated person-centered therapy, a psychotherapy approach that focuses on facilitating the client's self-actualizing tendency, which he considered the basic motive of all people.

One of the most revolutionary concepts to grow out of our clinical experience is the growing recognition that the innermost core of man's nature, the deepest layers of his personality, the base of his "animal nature," is positive in nature—is basically socialized, forward-moving, rational and realistic.

QUESTION

Which of these two perspectives on human nature resonates with you more, and why?

III. INNOCENT OR RIGHTEOUS?

To appreciate the Jewish perspective on the question of human nature, we will turn to its expression in Jewish law and contrast it with the secular legal system.

TEXT 5

Presumption of Innocence

Massachusetts District Court, Criminal Model Jury Instructions, January 2020

The law presumes the defendant to be innocent of (the charge) (all the charges) against him (her). This presumption of innocence is a rule of law that compels you to find the defendant not guilty unless and until the Commonwealth produces evidence, from whatever source, that proves that the defendant is guilty beyond a reasonable doubt. This burden of proof never shifts. The defendant is not required to call any witnesses or produce any evidence, since he (she) is presumed to be innocent.

The presumption of innocence stays with the defendant unless and until the evidence convinces you unanimously as a jury that the defendant is guilty beyond a reasonable doubt. It requires you to find the defendant not guilty unless his (her) guilt has been proved beyond a reasonable doubt.

TEXT 6

Presumption of Righteousness

Rabbi Shmuel de Medina, *Shu"t Maharashdam*,
Choshen Mishpat, Responsa 310

**RABBI SHMUEL BEN
MOSHE DE MEDINA
1506–1580**

Halachic decisor. A
resident of Thessaloniki,
Greece, Rabbi Shmuel
served as the head of
the local rabbinic court
and yeshiva. Known
for his firm halachic
positions and personal
humility, he was a leading
decider on halachic
inquiries from Italy and
the Balkan region. His
responsa were published
under the title *Shu"t
Maharashdam*, and they
have had a lasting effect
on rabbinical scholarship.

דָּבָר גָּלוּי וְיָדוּעַ שֶׁכָּל יִשְׂרָאֵל בְּחֶזְקַת כְּשֵׁרִים הֵם.

כְּמוֹ שֶׁאָנוּ אוֹמְרִים בִּבְהֵמָה בְּחַיֶּיהָ בְּחֶזְקַת אִסּוּר
עוֹמֶדֶת עַד שֶׁיִּוָּדַע לְךָ בַּמֶּה נִשְׁחַט וְיוֹצְאָה מֵחֶזְקַת
אִסּוּר אֵבֶר מִן הַחַי. נִשְׁחֲטָה, יָצְאָה מֵחֶזְקַת הָאִסּוּר
אֲשֶׁר הָיָה לָהּ וּבְחֶזְקַת הֶתֵּר עוֹמֶדֶת עַד שֶׁיִּוָּדַע לְךָ
בִּבְרוּר בַּמֶּה נִטְרַף כַּמְבֹאָר פֶּרֶק קַמָּא דְחֻלִּין.

כְּמוֹ כֵן, כָּל בֶּן יִשְׂרָאֵל עֲשָׂאוֹ ה' יָשָׁר מִתְּחִלַּת בְּרִיאָתוֹ
וּבְחֶזְקַת כָּשֵׁר עוֹמֵד עַד יִוָּדַע לְךָ בְּבֵרוּר בִּקֵּשׁ חֶשְׁבּוֹנוֹת
וְאָרְחוֹת עֲקַלְקַלוֹת לָצֵאת מִדֶּרֶךְ הָאֱמֶת וְהַיָּשָׁר.

It is clear and established that we are
all presumed to be righteous.

This is analogous to presumptions we use regarding
the kosher status of animals. As long as an animal
is alive it is forbidden for consumption, and it is
presumed to have remained in this state until we can
ascertain that it has been slaughtered properly. Once
the animal has been slaughtered properly, it is then
presumed to be kosher unless it is clearly proven
to be nonkosher due to a severe physical defect.

Similarly, G-d created each of us upright
and honest by nature. People retain this
presumption of righteousness unless it has

Learn from the
Lubavitcher Rebbe how
to find the good in every
person and situation:
myjli.com/beyondright

been clearly proven that they have chosen to veer from the way of truth and righteousness and follow a deceitful and crooked path.

QUESTIONS

1. With which of the two views regarding human nature is the secular legal principle in Text 5 compatible?

2. With which of the two views regarding human nature is the Jewish legal principle in Text 6 compatible?

Perhaps the oldest manuscript of the Talmud that has ever been discovered, this ancient vellum scroll fragment contains the text of tractate Chulin of the Babylonian Talmud 101a–105a, which discusses some of the laws of Kosher. The rare scroll, dated around the 10th century, is from the Cairo *geneizah* and may have been part of the texts copied by the Torah academies in Babylon to be sent to Jewish communities in other locations. (Cambridge University Library [T-S Misc.26.53.17])

TEXT 7

The Pure Soul

Siddur, Morning Blessings

אֱלֹקַי, נְשָׁמָה שֶׁנָּתַתָּ בִּי טְהוֹרָה הִיא. אַתָּה בְרָאתָהּ,
אַתָּה יְצַרְתָּהּ, אַתָּה נְפַחְתָּהּ בִּי, וְאַתָּה מְשַׁמְּרָהּ בְּקִרְבִּי.

My G-d, the soul that You have placed in me is
pure. You created it; You formed it; You breathed
it into me; and You preserve it within me.

SIDDUR

The siddur is the Jewish prayer book. It was originally developed by the sages of the Great Assembly in the 4th century BCE, and later reconstructed by Rabban Gamliel after the destruction of the Second Temple. Various authorities continued to add prayers, from then until contemporary times. It includes praise of G-d, requests for personal and national needs, selections from the Bible, and much else. Various Jewish communities have slightly different versions of the siddur.

SOUL DANCE
Yitzchok Moully, acrylic
and ink on canvas, 2012

TEXT 8

Foolish Spirits

Talmud, Sotah 3a

אֵין אָדָם עוֹבֵר עֲבֵרָה
אֶלָּא אִם כֵּן נִכְנַס בּוֹ רוּחַ שְׁטוּת.

People only transgress when they are
overcome by a spirit of foolishness.

BABYLONIAN TALMUD

A literary work of
monumental proportions
that draws upon the legal,
spiritual, intellectual,
ethical, and historical
traditions of Judaism.
The 37 tractates of the
Babylonian Talmud
contain the teachings of
the Jewish sages from
the period after the
destruction of the 2nd
Temple through the 5th
century CE. It has served
as the primary vehicle
for the transmission
of the Oral Law and
the education of Jews
over the centuries; it
is the entry point for
all subsequent legal,
ethical, and theological
Jewish scholarship.

PRAYING FIGURE
Creator unknown. Painted
iron figure made in the late
19th or early 20th century.
A spring enables the figure
to sway back and forth,
a traditional movement
during Jewish prayer. (The
Jewish Museum, New York)

IV. RIGHTEOUS TRUST

We now turn to explore how Judaism's positive view of human nature and belief in people's essential goodness are expressed in its legal system.

TEXT 9

Kosher Slaughter Qualifications

Maimonides, *Mishneh Torah*, Laws of Kosher Slaughter 4:1, 3–4

RABBI MOSHE
BEN MAIMON
(MAIMONIDES, RAMBAM)
1135–1204

Halachist, philosopher,
author, and physician.
Maimonides was born
in Córdoba, Spain. After
the conquest of Córdoba
by the Almohads, he fled
Spain and eventually
settled in Cairo, Egypt.
There, he became the
leader of the Jewish
community and served
as court physician to
the vizier of Egypt.
He is most noted for
authoring the *Mishneh
Torah*, an encyclopedic
arrangement of
Jewish law; and for his
philosophical work,
Guide for the Perplexed.
His rulings on Jewish
law are integral to
the formation of
Halachic consensus.

יִשְׂרָאֵל שֶׁאֵינוֹ יוֹדֵעַ חֲמִשָּׁה דְּבָרִים שֶׁמַּפְסִידִין אֶת הַשְּׁחִיטָה וְכַיּוֹצֵא בָּהֶן מֵהִלְכוֹת שְׁחִיטָה שֶׁבֵּאַרְנוּ, וְשָׁחַט בֵּינוֹ לְבֵין עַצְמוֹ, אָסוּר לֶאֱכֹל מִשְּׁחִיטָתוֹ . . .

יִשְׂרָאֵל שֶׁיּוֹדֵעַ הִלְכוֹת שְׁחִיטָה הֲרֵי זֶה לֹא יִשְׁחֹט בֵּינוֹ לְבֵין עַצְמוֹ לְכַתְּחִלָּה, עַד שֶׁיִּשְׁחֹט בִּפְנֵי חָכָם פְּעָמִים רַבּוֹת עַד שֶׁיִּהְיֶה רָגִיל וְזָרִיז . . .

הַיּוֹדֵעַ הִלְכוֹת שְׁחִיטָה וְשָׁחַט בִּפְנֵי חָכָם עַד שֶׁנַּעֲשָׂה רָגִיל הוּא הַנִּקְרָא מֻמְחֶה.

A Jew who doesn't know the laws of *shechitah* (kosher slaughter) may not slaughter. Any meat slaughtered by such a person is forbidden for consumption. . . .

Even a person who knows the laws of kosher slaughter should not slaughter alone before practicing many times under the supervision of an expert scholar and achieving proficiency in the technique. . . .

Only a person who is well-versed in the laws of *shechitah* and has practiced under expert supervision until achieving proficiency is considered a qualified expert.

TEXT 10

The Righteous Unknown

Maimonides, *Mishneh Torah*, Laws of Kosher Slaughter 4:7

הֲרֵי שֶׁרְאִינוּ יִשְׂרְאֵלִי מֵרְחוֹק שֶׁשָּׁחַט וְהָלַךְ לוֹ, וְלֹא יָדַעְנוּ אִם יוֹדֵעַ אִם אֵינוֹ יוֹדֵעַ, הֲרֵי זוֹ מֻתֶּרֶת . . . שֶׁרֹב הַמְּצוּיִין אֵצֶל שְׁחִיטָה מֻמְחִין הֵן.

If a Jew came and slaughtered an animal and left before we were able to determine whether or not he was a proficient practitioner, the meat may be consumed. . . .

The rationale for this law is that the majority of slaughter practitioners are experts.

TEXT 11

Individual Judgment

Rabbi Yosef Dov Soloveitchik, *Beit Halevi* 2:4

RABBI YOSEF DOV
SOLOVEITCHIK OF BRISK
1820–1892

Lithuanian rabbi and
Talmudic scholar;
known for his collection
of responsa and his
biblical commentary,
both titled *Beit Halevi*.
A great-grandson
of Rabbi Chaim of
Volozhin, Rabbi
Soloveitchik was
recognized as a child
prodigy. During the
course of his illustrious
career he served as
head of the yeshiva in
Volozhin, and as rabbi
in Slutsk and Brisk.

כָּל יִשְׂרָאֵל כֻּלָּם הֲרֵי הֵם אֶצְלֵנוּ בְּחֶזְקַת כְּשֵׁרִים בְּוַדַּאי,
וּבְוַדַּאי דְּחוֹשְׁשִׁים לְאִסּוּר נְבֵלָה. וְכָל מִי שֶׁחוֹשֵׁשׁ
לְאִסּוּר נְבֵלָה בְּוַדַּאי דְּלֹא יִשְׁחֹט אִם אֵינוֹ מֻמְחֶה.

וּמִשּׁוּם הָכִי לֹא שַׁיָּךְ כָּאן לוֹמַר סְמֹךְ מִעוּטָא לַחֲזָקָה. דַּהֲרֵי
בְּהַכְּשֵׁרִים מִיִּשְׂרָאֵל לֵיכָּא מִעוּטָא כְּלָל, וּלְמִעוּטָא דְּאֵינָן
כְּשֵׁרִים הֲרֵי אֵין לָחוּשׁ כְּלָל. דְּכָל אֶחָד מִיִּשְׂרָאֵל כָּל זְמַן שֶׁלֹּא
נֶחֱשַׁד לְפָנֵינוּ הֲרֵי הוּא אֶצְלֵנוּ בְּחֶזְקַת וַדַּאי כָּשֵׁר בְּלֹא שׁוּם
סָפֵק, וְלֹא מִטַּעַם רוּבָּא לְחוּדָא מַחְזְקִינָן לְכָל אֶחָד בְּכָשֵׁר.

דְּאַף עַל גַּב דְּבִכְלַל כָּל הָעוֹלָם אִיכָּא מִעוּט אֲנָשִׁים
חֲשׁוּדִים, מִכָּל מָקוֹם כָּל אֶחָד מִיִּשְׂרָאֵל שֶׁאֲנַחְנוּ דָנִים
עָלָיו הוּא אֶצְלֵנוּ בְּחֶזְקַת וַדַּאי כָּשֵׁר בְּלֹא שׁוּם סָפֵק.

We consider every Jew as certainly righteous. We
are certain that they are particular about the laws
of kosher *shechitah* (slaughter) and wouldn't
slaughter if they weren't a qualified expert.

As a result, we don't say that since there exists
a minority of nonexperts who slaughter, the
animal remains in its established nonkosher
status. Among righteous Jews there is not even
a minority that would act improperly. The
minority of unrighteous Jews isn't a factor
worthy of consideration because every Jew that
has not been established as suspect must be

considered as undoubtedly righteous. The presumption of righteousness is thus not just majority-based.

We know that there is an unrighteous minority present in the world at large. But every individual Jew that we are evaluating must be considered as certainly righteous without reservation.

The Righteous Suspect

Talmud, Shevu'ot 46a–b

רָאוּהוּ שֶׁהִטְמִין כֵּלִים תַּחַת כְּנָפָיו וְיָצָא וְאָמַר לְקוּחִין הֵן בְּיָדִי, אֵינוֹ נֶאֱמָן . . .

וְלֹא אֲמַרָן אֶלָּא זֶה אוֹמֵר שְׁאוּלִין וְזֶה אוֹמֵר לְקוּחִין. אֲבָל בִּגְנוּבִין, לָאו כָּל כְּמִנֵיהּ, לְאַחְזוּקֵי אִינִישׁ בְּגַנְבֵי לֹא מַחְזְקִינַן.

Witnesses saw a person enter another's house and leave with items concealed beneath his garments. The possessor of the items claims that he purchased them, while the owner of the house denies this. The law in this case is that the possessor is not believed. . . .

This principle only applies when the homeowner claims that the items in question were on loan, and the possessor claims that they were purchased. But if the homeowner claims that the items were stolen, his accusation is rejected, for we do not presume a person to be a thief without proof.

TEXT 13

Preempting Buyers

Talmud, Kidushin 59a

רַב גִּידֵל הֲוָה מְהַפִּיךְ בְּהַהִיא אַרְעָא. אֲזַל רַבִּי אַבָּא, זַבְנָהּ. אֲזַל רַב גִּידֵל קַבְלֵיהּ לְרַבִּי זֵירָא. אֲזַל רַבִּי זֵירָא וְקַבְלֵיהּ לְרַב יִצְחָק נַפְחָא. אָמַר לֵיהּ, הַמְתֵּן עַד שֶׁיַּעֲלֶה אֶצְלֵנוּ לָרֶגֶל.

כִּי סָלִיק, אַשְׁכְּחֵיהּ. אָמַר לֵיהּ, עָנִי מְהַפֵּךְ בַּחֲרָרָה וּבָא אַחֵר וּנְטָלָהּ הֵימֶנּוּ, מַאי.

אָמַר לֵיהּ, נִקְרָא רָשָׁע. וְאֶלָּא מַר מַאי טַעֲמָא עָבַד הָכִי.

אָמַר לֵיהּ, לֹא הֲוָה יָדַעְנָא.

Rabbi Gidel attempted to acquire a certain plot of land, but Rabbi Abba preempted him and purchased it. Rabbi Gidel complained about Rabbi Abba's actions to Rabbi Zeira, who relayed the complaint to Rabbi Yitzchak Nafcha. Rabbi Yitzchak Nafcha told them to wait until Rabbi Abba would visit him for the festival, at which point he would discuss the matter with him.

When Rabbi Abba arrived, Rabbi Yitzchak Nafcha asked him, "What is the law in a case whereby a pauper moves to acquire an ownerless loaf of bread that he found, but someone else comes along and preempts him?"

Rabbi Abba replied, "The one who took it away is referred to as wicked." Rabbi Yitzchak Nafcha pressed Rabbi Abba, "If so, why did you act in this way?

Rabbi Abba replied, "I did not know that Rabbi Gidel was trying to acquire the land."

THE WORLD'S OLDEST TRIBUNAL, DATING FROM MOSES: THE BETH DIN, OR COURT OF THE CHIEF RABBI

From the *Illustrated London News*, August 14, 1926, drawn by Brian de Grineau. The detailed drawings depict several proceedings of the court of Jewish law, headed at the time by Rabbi J. H. Hertz, the chief rabbi of the U.K. from 1913 until 1946, pictured in the center.

TEXT 14

Righteous in Spite

Rabbi Nisim of Gerona, Kidushin 51b

מִי שֶׁעָשָׂה שָׁלִיחַ לִקַּח לוֹ קַרְקַע וְהָלַךְ וּלְקָחוֹ
סְתָם, יָכוֹל לוֹמַר לְעַצְמִי לְקַחְתִּי.

וּמֵיהוּ, נִרְאָה לִי דְּדַוְקָא בְּקַרְקַע סְתָם. אֲבָל בְּקַרְקַע
מְיֻחָד, כֵּיוָן שֶׁהוּא מִנְהַג רָמָאִין כִּדְאִיתָא בְּפֶרֶק
הָאוֹמֵר (קִדּוּשִׁין נט, א) לֹא מָצֵי אָמַר, דִּשְׁאֵרִית
יִשְׂרָאֵל לֹא יַעֲשׂוּ עַוְלָה (צְפַנְיָה יג, ג).

A person appointed someone to serve as his agent to purchase a specific property. The agent purchased the property without specifying in the purchase agreement that he was doing so on behalf of the principal, and he now claims to have purchased it for himself in a personal capacity.

The law is that we reject the agent's claim, on the grounds that the Talmud (KIDUSHIN 59A) labels such an action as "deceitful conduct"—and we operate under the assumption that "the remnant of Israel will not commit an injustice" (ZEPHANIAH 13:3).

THERE'S MORE...

Jewish law even applies its presumption of righteousness to proven transgressors, as the Appendix (on p. 189) explains.

RABBI NISIM BEN REUVEN "THE RAN" OF GERONA 1320–1380

Influential talmudist and authority on Jewish law; among the last great Spanish talmudic scholars. Considered the outstanding Halachic authority of his generation, queries came to him from throughout the Diaspora. His works include commentaries on the Talmud and on Rabbi Yitzchak Alfasi's code, responsa literature, a commentary on the Bible, and a collection of sermons, *Derashot Haran*, which elucidates fundamentals of Judaism.

V. BEHAVIORAL RIGHTEOUSNESS

As demonstrated, Judaism nurtures a universally applied positivity bias, and this value guides the Jewish legal system. Does this require a leap of faith—a value based on purely religious and philosophical belief—or is it also supported by behavioral evidence?

TEXT 15

Test of Honesty

Pam Belluck, "Would You Return This Lost Wallet?"
The New York Times, June 20, 2019

Researchers planted 17,303 wallets in 355 cities on every continent except Antarctica. The American segment, conducted in 2015, involved 25 cities including Albuquerque, Chicago, Memphis and New York.

The wallets, transparent business card cases with contents instantly visible, contained three business cards with a male name common to that country (Dimitri Ivanov for Russia, Tono Hendrianta for Indonesia, Peter Kihiga for Kenya). The American names were Brad O'Brien, Brett Miller or Connor Baker.

Each business card listed an email address and identified the man as a freelance software engineer so people wouldn't try contacting employers.

Each wallet also contained a key and a handwritten grocery list in the native language: milk (or a locally analogous drink), bread, pasta (or rice or noodles), bananas. Some wallets had no money inside; some had $13.45 in local currency, adjusted to a comparable value for each country. . . .

Then they ran the experiment again in three countries (Poland, the United Kingdom and the United States), adding "big money" wallets containing $94.15.

EXERCISE 6.3

What percentage of people do you think would return the wallet in the three different scenarios?

a.   **No money**

b.   **$13.45**

c.   **$94.15**

FIGURE 6.1

Honesty Rates

Alain Cohn, et al., "Civic Honesty around the Globe,"
Science, vol. 365, Issue 6448 (July 5, 2019), pp. 70–73

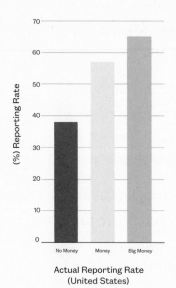

**Actual Reporting Rate
(United States)**

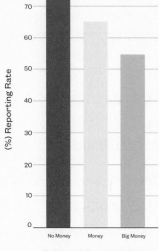

**Predicted Reporting Rate
(Non-Expert Sample)**

KEY POINTS

1   We have a natural tendency to judge ourselves favorably, a courtesy we typically fail to extend to others. Jewish values train us to extend our personal positive bias to others.

2   Judaism views all humans as essentially good by nature, on account of the pure divine soul we possess. Negative conduct is viewed as a foreign imposition on our basic nature.

3   Jewish law views individuals as righteous unless clearly proven otherwise. Unknown people are afforded more than the benefit of the doubt due to a lack of evidence; they are treated as certainly righteous based on the positive nature native to all humans.

4   In certain cases, Jewish law refuses to accept a person's own claim that they acted unethically, due to the underlying presumption of righteousness.

5   Behavioral studies demonstrate that people are typically more virtuous than we assume.

6   Judaism teaches us not to judge people based on statistics or beliefs regarding the broader public, but to assess others with a favorable eye based on their individual merits.

COURSE CONCLUSION

In the following lines, describe how this course is relevant to your life personally, and identify a specific area where you can implement one of the topics discussed.

Choosing the Better Option

Talmud, Chulin 4a

TEXT 16

יִשְׂרָאֵל מוּמָר אוֹכֵל נְבֵלוֹת לְתֵאָבוֹן, בּוֹדֵק
סַכִּין וְנוֹתֵן לוֹ, וּמֻתָּר לֶאֱכֹל מִשְּׁחִיטָתוֹ.

מַאי טַעֲמָא, כֵּיוָן דְּאִיכָּא הֶתֵּירָא וְאִיסוּרָא
לֹא שָׁבִיק הֶתֵּירָא וְאָכִיל אִיסּוּרָא.

אִי הָכִי, כִּי לֹא בָּדַק נַמִי, מִיטְרַח לֹא טָרַח.

A person that isn't particular about the laws of
kosher foods and willfully eats nonkosher meat
can still be trusted to slaughter an animal properly,
so long as the slaughtering knife was examined
and confirmed to be perfectly suitable for use.

In this case, the person has the option to slaughter
the animal properly or to slaughter the animal
improperly. We assume that the slaughterer
would not choose to intentionally slaughter
improperly if he can also do it properly.

It is nevertheless necessary to examine the knife
beforehand, because we don't trust someone
unscrupulous about the kosher laws to make the
effort of guaranteeing that the blade is fit for use.

Chazakah: Resolving Uncertainty

A *chazakah*, "presumption" (pl., *chazakot*), is a mechanism of Jewish law available for resolving uncertainty surrounding the legal status of persons or properties.

Chazakot come in various forms, with varying degrees of clout. The discussion surrounding their precise applications generates a generous portion of Jewish legal literature.

Seven of the primary forms of *chazakot* are presented below, each with a brief illustration of application.

Chezkat Kashrut

Individuals are assumed to be righteous unless proven otherwise.

Illustration

If *shechitah* (ritual slaughter) was performed on an animal by an individual whose identity and training are unknown, the slaughterer is presumed to be a properly trained expert and the meat is permitted for consumption. We assume that this person was upright, and therefore wouldn't engage in *shechitah* unless properly licensed to do so.

Chezkat Umdena

This category of *chazakah* includes presumptions Jewish law makes based on its assessment of human nature.

Illustration

A disputed and unproven claim of early debt repayment is dismissed in light of the assessment that the overwhelming majority of borrowers offer repayment at the designated dates or subsequently, but not in advance.

Chazakah Deme'ikara

When the current legal status of a particular entity is suddenly cast into doubt, this *chazakah* may be asserted to allow the entity to retain its *most recently* established, undisputed legal status.

Illustration

An animal was subject to *shechitah* (kosher slaughter), but the Halachic propriety of the *shechitah* is cast into doubt. In this case, the animal is deemed nonkosher for consumption by force of presumption, as follows: The act of *shechitah* having been cast into doubt, the animal reverts to its last known definite status, namely, its status while alive—living creatures being always *unfit* for consumption by Torah law.

Chezkat Mara Kama

When faced with conflicting claims of real property ownership, the last proven owner is presumed to be the rightful owner.

Illustration

A was a proven owner of real property. However, B claims that the property was sold to him by A. In this case, B must present the court with evidence of the sale, or evidence that the property was in his possession for three consecutive years with A's full knowledge and without any ownership challenge on the part of A. If B cannot present such evidence, the court relies on the *chazakah* to disregard B's claim—even if B is currently in possession of the property—and the property is restored to the most recent proven owner: A.

Chezkat Shalosh Pe'amim

When certain events occur three times, it creates an assumption of continuous repetition.

Illustration

If an individual owns an animal that has on three occasions inflicted harm on another animal, its owner must assume that the creature is dangerous and will repeatedly harm unless adequate safeguards are set in place. Consequently, if the owner fails to establish such safeguards and the animal causes further harm, the owner's lack of attention to an established *chazakah* pattern of conduct will cause his liability to increase significantly.

Chezkat Mitaltelin

An assumption of rightful ownership bestowed upon the current possessor of movable assets.

Illustration

X is found to be in possession of movable items, but Y delivers evidence that identifies Y as the original lawful owner of these items. Y claims that X borrowed the items but subsequently refused to return them. X insists, without presenting evidence, that the items were lawfully purchased from Y. Under the force of this *chazakah*, the court sides with X simply because the items are *currently* in that individual's possession.

Huchzak

An assumption based on existing public knowledge.

Illustration

When two individuals are known to the public as close relatives, Jewish law considers them as such unless proven otherwise.

Judging Favorably

A collection of Talmudic stories illustrating the value of judging others favorably.

Talmud, Shabbat 127b

Those who judge others favorably are themselves judged favorably. This truth is demonstrated by the following incident:

An inhabitant of the [Holy Land's] Upper Galilee region traveled south in search of work. He was hired to work for a southern homeowner for a three-year term. On the eve of Yom Kippur, he appealed to the homeowner, "Pay me my wages, so that I can go home and provide for my wife and children."

The homeowner replied, "I have no money."

The worker responded, "In that case, pay me my wages in the form of produce."

The homeowner replied, "I have none."

The worker pleaded, "Pay me my wages in the form of land."

The homeowner replied, "I have none."

The worker begged, "Then pay me my wages in the form of animals."

The homeowner replied, "I have none."

The worker implored, "If so, pay me my wages in the form of pillows or cushions."

Replied the homeowner, "I have none."

The worker slung his belongings over his shoulder and returned home dejected.

Shortly thereafter, following the festival of Sukkot, the homeowner took the worker's wages in his hand, along with three donkeys loaded with goods—a load of food stuffs, a load of beverages, and a load of assorted sweet delicacies—and traveled to his former employee's home. After they ate and drank, the homeowner paid the worker his wages.

The homeowner then questioned his former employee: "When you requested your wages and I replied that I had no money—of what did you suspect me?"

The worker replied, "I told myself that you may have recently encountered a golden opportunity to purchase underpriced merchandise, and used the funds set aside for my wages to purchase it. In that case, you would not have further available funds to pay me at such short notice."

The homeowner asked, "When you asked me to pay you with animals, and I replied that I have none—of what did you suspect me?"

The worker responded, "I thought to myself: perhaps the animals were leased to others."

The homeowner prodded, "When you asked me to pay you with land, and I claimed that I have no land—of what did you suspect me?"

The worker replied, "I thought to myself that perhaps the land was leased to others."

The homeowner asked, "When you asked me to pay you with produce, and I said that I have no produce—of what did you suspect me?"

The worker answered, "I reasoned that the produce may not have been properly tithed, and as a result, you were unable to let me have it."

The homeowner inquired, "When you asked me to pay you with pillows or cushions and I claimed to have none—of what did you suspect me?"

The worker responded, "I thought that you may have consecrated all your possessions to Heaven and therefore had nothing available."

The homeowner exclaimed, "By the Holy Temple's service! I swear that it was so. I had pledged all of my possessions to Heaven at the time, because of my son Hurkanos—I did not want him to benefit from my possessions because he refused to engage in Torah study. Then, when I came to my learned colleagues in the South, they annulled all of my vows. As for you, just as you judged me favorably, so may G-d judge you favorably."

Talmud, Sanhedrin 26a

Reish Lakish observed a Jewish man plowing a field. He exclaimed to the sages who accompanied him, "Look at this fellow who is plowing during the sabbatical year [in breach of the Torah's commandment to let the land lie fallow]!"

The sages responded, "Why assume that this man is transgressing the law? Perhaps he is a hired worker servicing a field that belongs to a non-Jew [who is not obligated in the sabbatical laws]."

Reish Lakish subsequently observed a man pruning vines in the vineyards. He exclaimed to the other sages, "Look at this fellow who is pruning vines during the sabbatical year!"

The sages retorted, "Why assume that this man is transgressing the law? Perhaps he is cutting the vines in order to use them [for a permissible, non-agricultural purpose, such] as a netting for an olive press."

Talmud, Taanit 21b

After hearing the praises of Abba the surgeon, Abaye sent a pair of rabbis to investigate the extent of Abba's righteousness.

When the rabbis arrived, Abba sat them down, fed them, and provided drinks. At night, he spread woolen rugs for them to sleep on.

In the morning, the visiting rabbis rolled up the rugs and took them, going out with them to the marketplace. They met their host Abba at the market and said to him, "Sir, please evaluate how much these rugs are worth and purchase them from us." Abba nominated their value. The rabbis countered, "Perhaps these rugs are worth more?" Abba replied, "This is the price I paid for them...." The rabbis then declared, "Indeed, these are your rugs! We took them from your house."

The rabbis pressed Abba, "Please tell us—of what did you suspect us when you discovered that we had taken the rugs this morning? Abba responded, "I told myself that you must have been working on an urgent case of ransoming Jewish captives but you were embarrassed to ask me for money directly."

The rabbis told Abba, "Now that you know, sir, please accept your rugs back." Abba demurred, "From the moment I concluded that you had taken the rugs for the purpose of redeeming captives I put them out of my mind and assigned them to charity."

Avot DeRabbi Natan, Nusach Bet, Chapter 19

A man once sent his son to a colleague to borrow a measure of wheat. When the son approached the man, the fellow was busy measuring wheat. The son announced, "My father would like to know whether you can lend him a measure of wheat." The man responded, "I don't own that amount of wheat."

The son returned to his father and related, "I met the fellow while he was measuring wheat, but he told me he does not have wheat to lend you." The father replied, "Perhaps the wheat he was measuring was part of the *maaser sheni* tithe [and he is forbidden to lend it to me]."

The father sent his son once more to the same fellow, this time to borrow a *maneh* [a small sum of money]. The son found the fellow counting money, and announced, "My father would like to know whether you can lend him a *maneh*." The man responded, "I don't own that amount of money."

The son returned to his father and reported, "I met him as he was counting money, but he told me he doesn't have money to lend you." The father explained, "Perhaps the money he was counting was part of a deposit he was holding for someone else."

Later, the father met the fellow in the marketplace. The fellow inquired, "Tell me, my friend: when you heard that your son came to me and observed me measuring wheat but that I declined to lend any of it—what did you say?" The father responded, "I said that perhaps the wheat you were measuring was part of your *maaser sheni* tithe." The man continued, "When you heard that your son found me counting money but that I refused to lend him any of it—what did you say?" Replied the father, "I said that perhaps the money is someone's deposit."

The man exclaimed, "Indeed! That is precisely the case. This is what our sages meant when they told us to judge every person favorably!"

Acknowledgments

We are grateful to the following individuals for their contributions to *Beyond Right*:

Flagship Director
RABBI SHMULY KARP

Curriculum Coordinator
RIVKI MOCKIN

Flagship Administrator
NAOMI HEBER

Author
RABBI SHMUEL SUPER

Editor
RABBI NAFTALI SILBERBERG

Advisory Board
RABBI LEVI DUBOV
RABBI SHIMON POSNER
RABBI SHOLOM RAICHIK
MRS. RIVKAH SLONIM
RABBI AVROHOM STERNBERG

Legal Research
RABBI MENDY KATZMAN

Judaic Research
RABBI YAKOV GERSHON
RABBI NOCHUM S. ZAJAC

Copywriter
RABBI YAAKOV PALEY

Proofreading
RACHEL MUSICANTE
YA'AKOVAH WEBER

Hebrew Punctuation
RABBI MOSHE WOLFF

Instructor Support
RABBI ISAAC ABELSKY
RABBI MENDEL ABELSKY

Design and Layout Administrator
SARA OSDOBA

Textbook and Marketing Design
CHAYA MUSHKA KANNER
RABBI LEVI WEINGARTEN

Textbook Layout
RIVKY FIELDSTEEL
SHAYNA GROSH
RABBI ZALMAN KORF

Imagery
SARA ROSENBLUM

Permissions
SHULAMIS NADLER

Publication and Distribution
RABBI MENDEL SIROTA
RABBI LEVI GOLDSHMID

Branding and Marketing
AVI WEBB

PowerPoint Presentations
CHANIE DENBURG
MUSHKA DRUK
MUSHKA GOLDFARB

Course Videos
GETZY RASKIN
MOSHE RASKIN

Key Points Videos
RABBI MOTTI KLEIN

We are immensely grateful for the encouragement of JLI's visionary chairman, and vice-chairman of *Merkos L'Inyonei Chinuch*—Lubavitch World Headquarters, **Rabbi Moshe Kotlarsky**. Rabbi Kotlarsky has been highly instrumental in building the infrastructure for the expansion of Chabad's international network and is also the architect of scores of initiatives and services to help Chabad representatives across the globe succeed in their mission. We are blessed to have the unwavering support of JLI's principal benefactor, **Mr. George Rohr**, who is fully invested in our work, continues to be instrumental in JLI's monumental growth and expansion, and is largely responsible for the Jewish renaissance that is being spearheaded by JLI and its affiliates across the globe.

The commitment and sage direction of JLI's dedicated Executive Board—**Rabbis Chaim Block, Hesh Epstein, Ronnie Fine, Yosef Gansburg, Shmuel Kaplan, Yisrael Rice**, and **Avrohom Sternberg**—and the countless hours they devote to the development of JLI are what drive the vision, growth, and tremendous success of the organization.

Finally, JLI represents an incredible partnership of more than 1,600 *shluchim* and *shluchot* in more than 1,000 locations across the globe, who contribute their time and talent to further Jewish adult education. We thank them for generously sharing feedback and making suggestions that steer JLI's development and growth. They are our most valuable critics and our most cherished contributors.

Inspired by the call of the **Lubavitcher Rebbe**, of righteous memory, it is the mandate of the Rohr JLI to provide a community of learning for all Jews throughout the world, where they can participate in their precious heritage of Torah learning and experience its rewards. May this course succeed in fulfilling this sacred charge!

On behalf of the Rohr Jewish Learning Institute,

RABBI EFRAIM MINTZ
Executive Director

RABBI YISRAEL RICE
Chairman, Editorial Board

11 Nisan, 5782

The Rohr Jewish Learning Institute

AN AFFILIATE OF MERKOS L'INYONEI CHINUCH,
THE EDUCATIONAL ARM OF THE CHABAD-LUBAVITCH MOVEMENT
832 EASTERN PARKWAY, BROOKLYN, NY 11213

CHAIRMAN
Rabbi Moshe Kotlarsky
Lubavitch World Headquarters

PRINCIPAL BENEFACTOR
Mr. George Rohr
New York, NY

EXECUTIVE DIRECTOR
Rabbi Efraim Mintz

EXECUTIVE COMMITTEE
Rabbi Chaim Block
S. Antonio, TX

Rabbi Hesh Epstein
Columbia, SC

Rabbi Ronnie Fine
Montreal, QC

Rabbi Yosef Gansburg
Toronto, ON

Rabbi Shmuel Kaplan
Potomac, MD

Rabbi Yisrael Rice
S. Rafael, CA

Rabbi Avrohom Sternberg
New London, CT

ADMINISTRATION
Rabbi Mendel Kotlarsky

ADMINISTRATOR
Rabbi Dubi Rabinowitz

ADVISORY BOARD OF GOVERNORS
George Rohr
New York, NY

Yaacov and Karen Cohen
Potomac, MD

Yitzchok and Julie Gniwisch
Montreal, QC

Barbara Hines
Aspen, CO

Ellen Marks
S. Diego, CA

David Mintz, OBM
Tenafly, NJ

Dr. Stephen F. Serbin
Columbia, SC

Leonard A. Wien, Jr.
Miami Beach, FL

ACADEMIC ADVISORY BOARD
Dr. Lewis Glinert
Professor of Hebraic Studies and Linguistics
Dartmouth College

Rabbi Edward Reichman, M.D.
Professor of Emergency Medicine
Albert Einstein College of Medicine

Dr. Jonathan Sarna
Professor of American Jewish History
Brandeis University

Dr. Lawrence H. Schiffman
Professor of Hebrew and Judaic Studies
New York University

EDUCATIONAL CONSULTANTS
Mr. Michael Brandwein
Lincolnshire, IL
Speech and Communication Expert

Dr. Andrew Effrat
Amherst, MA
Professor, School of Education
University of Massachusetts, Amherst

Dr. David Pelcovitz
New York, NY
Professor of Education and Psychology
Yeshiva University

Dr. Chana Silberstein
Ithaca, NY

Dr. Casey Skvorc
Washington, DC
National Institutes of Health

RABBINIC ADVISORY BOARD
Rabbi Nissan Mangel
Brooklyn, NY

Rabbi Yossi Shusterman
Beverly Hills, CA
SENIOR RABBINIC ADVISORS

Rabbi Mordechai Farkash
Bellevue, WA

Rabbi Mendel Lipskier
Sherman Oaks, CA

Rabbi Avrohom Sternberg
New London, CT

CURRICULUM DEVELOPMENT

Rabbi Mordechai Dinerman
Rabbi Naftali Silberberg
EDITORS IN CHIEF

Rabbi Shmuel Klatzkin, PhD
ACADEMIC CONSULTANT

Rabbi Yanki Tauber
COURSE DESIGNER

Rabbi Chaim Fieldsteel
Rabbi Eliezer Gurkow
Rabbi Shmuel Super
Rabbi Menashe Wolf
CURRICULUM AUTHORS

Rabbi Yaakov Paley
Rabbi Boruch Werdiger
WRITERS

Rabbi Ahrele Loschak
EDITOR, TORAH STUDIES

Rabbi Mendel Glazman
Mrs. Mushka Grossbaum
Rabbi Zalman Margolin
Rabbi Mendy Rabinowitz
Mrs. Mushka Rabinowitz
Rabbi Moshe Wolff
EDITORIAL SUPPORT

Rabbi Shmuel Gomes
Rabbi Yakov Gershon
RESEARCH

Rabbi Michoel Lipskier
Rabbi Mendel Rubin
EXPERIENTIAL LEARNING

Mrs. Rivki Mockin
CONTENT COORDINATOR

MARKETING AND BRANDING

Rabbi Zalman Abraham
DIRECTOR

Avi Webb
BRAND COPYWRITER

Ms. Rochel Karp
Ms. Sara Osdoba
DESIGN ADMINISTRATORS

Mrs. Chaya Mushka Kanner
Ms. Estie Ravnoy
Mrs. Shifra Tauber
Rabbi Levi Weingarten
GRAPHIC DESIGN

Mrs. Rivky Fieldsteel
Mrs. Shayna Grosh
Rabbi Motti Klein
Rabbi Zalman Korf
Rabbi Moshe Wolff
PUBLICATION DESIGN

Lazer Cohen
Yosef Feigelstock
Menachem Klein
Mrs. Basya Stevenson
Ms. Baila Vogel
SOCIAL MEDIA

Rabbi Yaakov Paley
COPYWRITER

Rabbi Yossi Grossbaum
Rabbi Mendel Lifshitz
Rabbi Shraga Sherman
Rabbi Ari Sollish
Rabbi Mendel Teldon
MARKETING COMMITTEE

MARKETING CONSULTANTS

Alan Rosenspan
ALAN ROSENSPAN & ASSOCIATES
Sharon, MA

Gary Wexler
PASSION MARKETING
Los Angeles, CA

JLI CENTRAL

Rabbi Isaac Abelsky
Rabbi Mendel Abelsky
Mrs. Adina Lerman
Ms. Mushka Majeski
Ms. Mimi Rabinowitz
Mrs. Aliza Scheinfeld
ADMINISTRATION

Ms. Liba Leah Gutnick
Rabbi Motti Klein
Mrs. Sara Rosenblum
Rabbi Shlomie Tenenbaum
Rabbi Chaim Zippel
PROJECT MANAGERS

Mrs. Mindy Wallach
AFFILIATE ORIENTATION

Mrs. Bunia Chazan
Mrs. Chanie Denburg
Mrs. Mushka Druk
Mrs. Mushka Goldfarb
Mrs. Baila Goldstein
Rabbi Motti Klein
Getzy Raskin
Moshe Raskin
MULTIMEDIA DEVELOPMENT

Rabbi Mendel Ashkenazi
Yoni Ben-Oni
Rabbi Mendy Elishevitz
Mendel Grossbaum
Ms. Danny Hess
Ms. Mushkie Lent
Rabbi Aron Liberow
Mrs. Chana Weinbaum
ONLINE DIVISION

Mrs. Ya'akovah Weber
LEAD PROOFREADER

Mrs. Rachel Musicante
PROOFREADER

Rabbi Levi Goldshmid
Rabbi Mendel Sirota
PRINTING AND DISTRIBUTION

Mrs. Musie Liberow
Mrs. Shaina B. Mintz
Mrs. Shulamis Nadler
ACCOUNTING

Ms. Chaya Mintz
Mrs. Shulamis Nadler
Mrs. Mindy Wallach
CONTINUING EDUCATION

JLI FLAGSHIP

Rabbi Yisrael Rice
CHAIRMAN

Rabbi Shmuly Karp
DIRECTOR

Mrs. Naomi Heber
PROJECT MANAGER

PAST FLAGSHIP AUTHORS

Rabbi Yitzchak M. Kagan
of blessed memory

Rabbi Zalman Abraham
Brooklyn, NY

Rabbi Berel Bell
Montreal, QC

Rabbi Nissan D. Dubov
London, UK

Rabbi Tzvi Freeman
Toronto, ON

Rabbi Eliezer Gurkow
London, ON

Rabbi Aaron Herman
Pittsburgh, PA

Rabbi Simon Jacobson
New York, NY

Rabbi Chaim D. Kagan, PhD
Monsey, NY

Rabbi Shmuel Klatzkin, PhD
Dayton, OH

Rabbi Nochum Mangel
Dayton, OH

Rabbi Moshe Miller
Chicago, IL

Rabbi Yosef Paltiel
Brooklyn, NY

Rabbi Yehuda Pink
Solihull, UK

Rabbi Yisrael Rice
S. Rafael, CA

Rabbi Eli Silberstein
Ithaca, NY

Mrs. Rivkah Slonim
Binghamton, NY

Rabbi Avrohom Sternberg
New London, CT

Rabbi Shais Taub
Cedarhurst, NY

Rabbi Shlomo Yaffe
Longmeadow, MA

ROSH CHODESH SOCIETY

Rabbi Shmuel Kaplan
CHAIRMAN

Mrs. Shaindy Jacobson
DIRECTOR

Mrs. Chana Dechter
ADMINISTRATOR

Mrs. Malky Bitton
Mrs. Shula Bryski
Mrs. Chanie Wilhelm
EDITORIAL BOARD

Mrs. Devorah Kornfeld
Mrs. Chana Lipskar
Mrs. Chana Alte Mangel
Mrs. Ahuva New
Mrs. Dinie Rapoport
Mrs. Sorah Shemtov
Mrs. Binie Tenenbaum
Mrs. Yehudis Wolvovsky
STEERING COMMITTEE

JLI TEENS

*In Partnership with CTeen:
Chabad Teen Network*

Rabbi Chaim Block
CHAIRMAN

Rabbi Shlomie Tenenbaum
DIRECTOR

TORAH STUDIES

Rabbi Yosef Gansburg
CHAIRMAN

Rabbi Shlomie Tenenbaum
PROJECT MANAGER

Rabbi Ahrele Loschak
EDITOR

Rabbi Levi Fogelman
Rabbi Yaacov Halperin
Rabbi Nechemia Schusterman
Rabbi Ari Sollish
STEERING COMMITTEE

SINAI SCHOLARS SOCIETY

In Partnership with Chabad on Campus

Rabbi Menachem Schmidt
CHAIRMAN

Rabbi Dubi Rabinowitz
DIRECTOR

Ms. Chanie Chesney
Ms. Mussi Rabinowitz
Mrs. Manya Sperlin
Mrs. Basya Stevenson
COORDINATORS

Mrs. Devorah Zlatopolsky
ADMINISTRATOR

Rabbi Shlomie Chein
VICE PRESIDENT STUDENT ENGAGEMENT,
CHABAD ON CAMPUS INTERNATIONAL

Rabbi Yossy Gordon
Rabbi Efraim Mintz
Rabbi Menachem Schmidt
Rabbi Avi Weinstein
EXECUTIVE COMMITTEE

Rabbi Levi Friedman
Rabbi Chaim Leib Hilel
Rabbi Yossi Lazaroff
Rabbi Levi Raichik
Rabbi Shmuel Tiechtel
Rabbi Shmuly Weiss
STEERING COMMITTEE

THE WELLNESS INSTITUTE

Adina Lerman
ADMINISTRATOR

Rabbi Zalman Abraham
VISION AND STRATEGIC PLANNING

Pamela Dubin
IMPACT ANALYSIS

Jeffrey Wengrofsky
ACADEMIC LIAISON

Mindy Wallach
ADMINISTRATIVE SPECIALIST

Esty Levin
Mushky Lipskier
PROJECT MANAGERS

Dina Zarchi
NETWORKING AND DEVELOPMENT

Shayna Horvath
PROJECT L'CHAIM COORDINATOR

CLINICAL ADVISORY BOARD

Sigrid Frandsen-Pechenik, PSY.D.
CLINICAL DIRECTOR

Kammarauche Asuzu, M.D., M.H.S.
Ryan G. Beale, MA, TLLP
David A. Brent, M.D.
Gittel Francis, LMSW
Jill Harkavy-Friedman, PhD
Madelyn S. Gould, PhD, M.P.H.
Lisa Jacobs, M.D., MBA
Thomas Joiner, PhD
E. David Klonsky, PhD
Bella Schanzer, M.D.
Jonathan Singer, PhD, LCSW
Casey Skvorc, PhD, JD
Darcy Wallen, LCSW, PC

JLI INTERNATIONAL

Rabbi Avrohom Sternberg
CHAIRMAN

Rabbi Dubi Rabinowitz
DIRECTOR

Rabbi Berry Piekarski
ADMINISTRATOR

Rabbi Eli Wolf
ADMINISTRATOR, JLI IN THE CIS
*In Partnership with the Federation
of Jewish Communities of the CIS*

Rabbi Shevach Zlatopolsky
EDITOR, JLI IN THE CIS

Rabbi Nochum Schapiro
REGIONAL REPRESENTATIVE, AUSTRALIA

Rabbi Avraham Golovacheov
REGIONAL REPRESENTATIVE, GERMANY

Rabbi Shmuel Katzman
REGIONAL REPRESENTATIVE,
NETHERLANDS

Rabbi Avrohom Steinmetz
REGIONAL REPRESENTATIVE, BRAZIL

Rabbi Bentzi Sudak
REGIONAL REPRESENTATIVE,
UNITED KINGDOM

Rabbi Shlomo Cohen
FRENCH COORDINATOR,
REGIONAL REPRESENTATIVE

NATIONAL JEWISH RETREAT

Rabbi Hesh Epstein
CHAIRMAN

Mrs. Shaina B. Mintz
DIRECTOR

Bruce Backman
HOTEL LIAISON

Rabbi Menachem Klein
PROGRAM COORDINATOR

Rabbi Shmuly Karp
Rabbi Chaim Zippel
SHLUCHIM LIAISONS

Rabbi Mendel Rosenfeld
LOGISTICS COORDINATOR

Ms. Rochel Karp
Mrs. Aliza Scheinfeld
SERVICE AND SUPPORT

JLI LAND & SPIRIT
Israel Experience

Rabbi Shmuly Karp
DIRECTOR

Rabbi Levi Goldshmid
SHLUCHIM LIAISON

Mrs. Shaina B. Mintz
ADMINISTRATOR

Rabbi Yechiel Baitelman
Rabbi Dovid Flinkenstein
Rabbi Chanoch Kaplan
Rabbi Levi Klein
Rabbi Mendy Mangel
Rabbi Sholom Raichik
STEERING COMMITTEE

SHABBAT IN THE HEIGHTS

Rabbi Shmuly Karp
DIRECTOR

Mrs. Shulamis Nadler
SERVICE AND SUPPORT

Rabbi Chaim Hanoka
CHAIRMAN

Rabbi Mordechai Dinerman
Rabbi Zalman Marcus
STEERING COMMITTEE

MYSHIUR
Advanced Learning Initiative

Rabbi Shmuel Kaplan
CHAIRMAN

Rabbi Shlomie Tenenbaum
ADMINISTRATOR

TORAHCAFE.COM
ONLINE LEARNING

Rabbi Mendy Elishevitz
WEBSITE DEVELOPMENT

Moshe Levin
CONTENT MANAGER

Mendel Laine
FILMING

MACHON SHMUEL
The Sami Rohr Research Institute

Rabbi Zalman Korf
ADMINISTRATOR

Rabbi Moshe Miller
Rabbi Gedalya Oberlander
Rabbi Chaim Rapoport
Rabbi Levi Yitzchak Raskin
Rabbi Chaim Schapiro
RABBINIC ADVISORY BOARD

Rabbi Yakov Gershon
RESEARCH FELLOW

FOUNDING DEPARTMENT HEADS

Rabbi Mendel Bell
Rabbi Zalman Charytan
Rabbi Mendel Druk
Rabbi Menachem Gansburg
Rabbi Meir Hecht
Rabbi Levi Kaplan
Rabbi Yoni Katz
Rabbi Chaim Zalman Levy
Rabbi Benny Rapoport
Dr. Chana Silberstein
Rabbi Elchonon Tenenbaum
Rabbi Mendy Weg

JLI Chapter Directory

ALABAMA

BIRMINGHAM
Rabbi Yossi Friedman............................205.970.0100

MOBILE
Rabbi Yosef Goldwasser........................251.265.1213

ALASKA

ANCHORAGE
Rabbi Yosef Greenberg
Rabbi Mendy Greenberg........................907.357.8770

ARIZONA

CHANDLER
Rabbi Mendy Deitsch.............................480.855.4333

FLAGSTAFF
Rabbi Dovie Shapiro..............................928.255.5756

FOUNTAIN HILLS
Rabbi Mendy Lipskier............................480.776.4763

ORO VALLEY
Rabbi Ephraim Zimmerman....................520.477.8672

PARADISE VALLEY
Rabbi Shlomo Levertov..........................480.788.9310

PHOENIX
Rabbi Dovber Dechter............................347.410.0785
Rabbi Zalman Levertov
Rabbi Yossi Friedman.............................602.944.2753

SCOTTSDALE
Rabbi Yossi Levertov.............................480.998.1410

SEDONA
Rabbi Mendel Kessler.............................928.985.0667

TUCSON
Rabbi Yehuda Ceitlin.............................520.881.7956

ARKANSAS

LITTLE ROCK
Rabbi Pinchus Ciment.............................501.217.0053

CALIFORNIA

AGOURA HILLS
Rabbi Moshe Bryski................................818.516.0444

ALAMEDA
Rabbi Meir Shmotkin..............................510.640.2590

BAKERSFIELD
Rabbi Shmuli Schlanger..........................661.834.1512

BEL AIR
Rabbi Chaim Mentz................................310.475.5311

BURBANK
Rabbi Shmuly Kornfeld...........................818.954.0070

CARLSBAD
Rabbi Yeruchem Eilfort
Mrs. Nechama Eilfort..............................760.943.8891

CHATSWORTH
Rabbi Yossi Spritzer...............................818.307.9907

CONCORD
Rabbi Berel Kesselman............................925.326.1613

CONTRA COSTA
Rabbi Dovber Berkowitz..........................925.937.4101

DANA POINT
Rabbi Eli Goorevitch...............................949.290.0628

DANVILLE
Rabbi Shmuli Raitman............................213.447.6694

EMERYVILLE
Rabbi Menachem Blank..........................510.859.8808

ENCINO
Rabbi Aryeh Herzog................................818.784.9986
Chapter founded by Rabbi Joshua Gordon, OBM

FOLSOM
Rabbi Yossi Grossbaum...........................916.608.9811

FREMONT
Rabbi Moshe Fuss..................................510.300.4090

GLENDALE
Rabbi Simcha Backman...........................818.240.2750

HOLLYWOOD
Rabbi Zalman Partouche 818.964.9428

HUNTINGTON BEACH
Rabbi Aron David Berkowitz 714.846.2285

LAGUNA NIGUEL
Rabbi Mendy Paltiel 949.831.7701

LA JOLLA
Rabbi Baruch Shalom Ezagui 858.455.5433

LAKE BALBOA
Rabbi Eli Gurary 347.403.6734

LOMITA
Rabbi Sholom Pinson 310.326.8234

LONG BEACH
Rabbi Abba Perelmuter 562.773.1350

LOS ANGELES
Rabbi Yossi Elifort 310.515.5310
Rabbi Leibel Korf 323.660.5177
Rabbi Zalmy Labkowsky 213.618.9486
Rabbi Mendel Zajac 310.770.9051

MALIBU
Rabbi Levi Cunin 310.456.6588

MARINA DEL REY
Rabbi Danny Yiftach-Hashem
Rabbi Dovid Yiftach 310.859.0770

MAR VISTA
Rabbi Shimon Simpson 646.401.2354

NEWHALL
Rabbi Choni Marosov 661.254.3434

NORTHRIDGE
Rabbi Eli Rivkin 818.368.3937

OJAI
Rabbi Mordechai Nemtzov 805.613.7181

PACIFIC PALISADES
Rabbi Zushe Cunin 310.454.7783

PALO ALTO
Rabbi Menachem Landa 415.418.4768
Rabbi Yosef Levin
Rabbi Ber Rosenblatt 650.424.9800

PASADENA
Rabbi Zushe Rivkin 626.788.3343

PLEASANTON
Rabbi Josh Zebberman 925.846.0700

POWAY
Rabbi Mendel Goldstein 858.208.6613

RANCHO CUCAMONGA
Rabbi Sholom Ber Harlig 909.949.4553

RANCHO MIRAGE
Rabbi Shimon H. Posner 760.770.7785

RANCHO PALOS VERDES
Rabbi Yitzchok Magalnic 310.544.5544

RANCHO S. FE
Rabbi Levi Raskin 858.756.7571

REDONDO BEACH
Rabbi Yossi Mintz
Rabbi Zalman Gordon 310.214.4999

RIVERSIDE
Rabbi Shmuel Fuss 951.329.2747

S. CLEMENTE
Rabbi Menachem M. Slavin 949.489.0723

S. CRUZ
Rabbi Yochanan Friedman 831.454.0101

S. DIEGO
Rabbi Rafi Andrusier 619.387.8770
Rabbi Yechiel Cagen 832.216.1534

S. FRANCISCO
Rebbetzin Mattie Pil 415.933.4310
Rabbi Gedalia Potash 415.648.8000
Rabbi Shlomo Zarchi 415.752.2866

S. MATEO
Rabbi Yossi Marcus 650.341.4510

S. RAFAEL
Rabbi Yisrael Rice 415.492.1666

SHERMAN OAKS
Rabbi Nachman Abend 818.989.9539

SONOMA
Rabbi Mendel Wolvovsky 707.292.6221

SOUTH LAKE TAHOE
Rabbi Mordechai Richler 530.539.4363

SUNNYVALE
Rabbi Yisroel Hecht 408.720.0553

TEMECULA
Rabbi Yonason Abrams 951.234.4196

TUSTIN
Rabbi Yehoshua Eliezrie 714.508.2150

VACAVILLE
Rabbi Chaim Zaklos 707.592.5300

WEST HILLS
Rabbi Avi Rabin 818.337.4544

WEST HOLLYWOOD
Rabbi Mordechai Kirschenbaum 310.691.9988

WEST LOS ANGELES
Rabbi Mordechai Zaetz 424.652.8742

YORBA LINDA
Rabbi Dovid Eliezrie 714.693.0770

COLORADO

ASPEN
Rabbi Mendel Mintz 970.544.3770

DENVER
Rabbi Yossi Serebryanski 303.744.9699
Rabbi Mendel Popack 720.515.4337
Rabbi Mendy Sirota 720.940.3716

FORT COLLINS
Rabbi Yerachmiel Gorelik 970.407.1613

HIGHLANDS RANCH
Rabbi Avraham Mintz 303.694.9119

LONGMONT
Rabbi Yakov Borenstein 303.678.7595

VAIL
Rabbi Dovid Mintz 970.476.7887

WESTMINSTER
Rabbi Benjy Brackman 303.429.5177

CONNECTICUT

FAIRFIELD
Rabbi Shlame Landa 203.373.7551

GREENWICH
Rabbi Yossi Deren
Rabbi Menachem Feldman 203.629.9059

HAMDEN
Rabbi Moshe Hecht 203.635.7268

MILFORD
Rabbi Schneur Wilhelm 203.887.7603

NEW HAVEN
Rabbi Mendy Hecht 203.589.5375
Rabbi Chanoch Wineberg 203.479.0313

NEW LONDON
Rabbi Avrohom Sternberg 860.437.8000

STAMFORD
Rabbi Yisrael Deren
Rabbi Levi Mendelow 203.3.CHABAD

WESTPORT
Rabbi Yehuda Kantor 561.460.3758

WEST HARTFORD
Rabbi Shaya Gopin 860.232.1116

SHELTON
Rabbi Schneur Brook 203.364.4149

DELAWARE

WILMINGTON
Rabbi Chuni Vogel 302.529.9900

DISTRICT OF COLUMBIA

WASHINGTON
Rabbi Levi Shemtov
Rabbi Yitzy Ceitlin 202.332.5600

FLORIDA

ALTAMONTE SPRINGS
Rabbi Mendy Bronstein 407.280.0535

BAL HARBOUR
Rabbi Dov Schochet 305.868.1411

BOCA RATON
Rabbi Zalman Bukiet 561.487.2934
Rabbi Arele Gopin 561.994.6257
Rabbi Moishe Denburg 561.526.5760
Rabbi Ruvi New 561.394.9770

BONITA SPRINGS
Rabbi Mendy Greenberg 239.949.6900

BOYNTON BEACH
Rabbi Yosef Yitzchok Raichik 561.732.4633

BRADENTON
Rabbi Menachem Bukiet 941.388.9656

CAPE CORAL
Rabbi Yossi Labkowski 239.963.4770

CORAL GABLES
Rabbi Avrohom Stolik 305.490.7572

CORAL SPRINGS
Rabbi Yankie Denburg 954.471.8646

CUTLER BAY
Rabbi Yossi Wolff 305.975.6680

DAVIE
Rabbi Aryeh Schwartz 954.376.9973

DELRAY BEACH
Rabbi Yaakov Perman 561.666.2770

FISHER ISLAND
Rabbi Efraim Brody 347.325.1913

FLEMING ISLAND
Rabbi Shmuly Feldman 904.290.1017

FORT LAUDERDALE
Rabbi Yitzchok Naparstek 954.568.1190

HALLANDALE BEACH
Rabbi Mordy Feiner 954.458.1877

HOLLYWOOD
Rabbi Leibel Kudan 954.801.3367

JUPITER
Rabbi Berel Barash 561.317.0968

KENDALL
Rabbi Yossi Harlig 305.234.5654

KEY BISCAYNE
Rabbi Avremel Caroline 305.365.6744

LAUDERHILL
Rabbi Shmuel Heidingsfeld 323.877.7703

LONGWOOD
Rabbi Yanky Majesky 407.636.5994

MAITLAND
Rabbi Sholom Dubov
Rabbi Levik Dubov 470.644.2500

MARION COUNTY
Rabbi Yossi Hecht 352.330.4466

MIAMI
Rabbi Mendy Cheruty 305.219.3353
Rabbi Yakov Fellig 305.445.5444

MIAMI BEACH
Rabbi Yisroel Frankforter 305.534.3895

N. MIAMI BEACH
Rabbi Eli Laufer 305.770.4412

ORLANDO
Rabbi Yosef Konikov 407.354.3660

ORMOND BEACH
Rabbi Asher Farkash 386.672.9300

PALM CITY
Rabbi Shlomo Uminer 772.485.5501

PALM BEACH
Rabbi Zalman Levitin 561.659.3884

PALM BEACH GARDENS
Rabbi Dovid Vigler 561.624.2223

PALM HARBOR
Rabbi Pinchas Adler 727.789.0408

PARKLAND
Rabbi Mendy Gutnick 954.600.6991

PEMBROKE PINES
Rabbi Mordechai Andrusier 954.874.2280

PLANTATION
Rabbi Pinchas Taylor 954.644.9177

PONTE VEDRA BEACH
Rabbi Nochum Kurinsky 904.543.9301

ROYAL PALM BEACH
Rabbi Nachmen Zeev Schtroks 561.714.1692

S. AUGUSTINE
Rabbi Levi Vogel 904.521.8664

S. JOHNS
Rabbi Mendel Sharfstein 347.461.3765

SARASOTA
Rabbi Chaim Shaul Steinmetz 941.925.0770

SATELLITE BEACH
Rabbi Zvi Konikov 321.777.2770

SINGER ISLAND
Rabbi Berel Namdar 347.276.6985

SOUTH PALM BEACH
Rabbi Leibel Stolik 561.889.3499

SOUTH TAMPA
Rabbi Mendy Dubrowski 813.922.1723

SOUTHWEST BROWARD COUNTY
Rabbi Aryeh Schwartz 954.252.1770

SUNNY ISLES BEACH
Rabbi Alexander Kaller 305.803.5315

SURFSIDE
Rabbi Dov Schochet 305.790.8294

TAMARAC
Rabbi Kopel Silberberg 954.882.7434

VENICE
Rabbi Sholom Ber Schmerling 941.330.4477

WESLEY CHAPEL
Rabbi Mendy Yarmush
Rabbi Mendel Friedman 813.731.2977

WEST PALM BEACH
Rabbi Yoel Gancz 561.659.7770

WESTON
Rabbi Yisroel Spalter 954.349.6565

GEORGIA

ALPHARETTA
Rabbi Hirshy Minkowicz 770.410.9000

ATLANTA
Rabbi Yossi New
Rabbi Isser New 404.843.2464
Rabbi Alexander Piekarski 678.267.6418

ATLANTA: INTOWN
Rabbi Eliyahu Schusterman
Rabbi Ari Sollish 404.898.0434

CUMMING
Rabbi Levi Mentz 310.666.2218

GWINNETT
Rabbi Yossi Lerman 678.595.0196

MARIETTA
Rabbi Ephraim Silverman 770.565.4412

HAWAII

KAPA'A
Rabbi Michoel Goldman 808.647.4293

IDAHO

BOISE
Rabbi Mendel Lifshitz 208.853.9200

ILLINOIS

ARLINGTON HEIGHTS
Rabbi Yaakov Kotlarsky 224.357.7002

CHAMPAIGN
Rabbi Dovid Tiechtel 217.355.8672

CHICAGO
Rabbi Meir Hecht 312.714.4655
Rabbi Dovid Kotlarsky 773.495.7127
Rabbi Mordechai Gershon 773.412.5189
Rabbi Yosef Moscowitz 773.772.3770
Rabbi Levi Notik 773.274.5123

DES PLAINES
Rabbi Lazer Hershkovich 224.392.4442

ELGIN
Rabbi Mendel Shemtov 847.440.4486

GLENVIEW
Rabbi Yishaya Benjaminson 847.910.1738

GURNEE
Rabbi Sholom Tenenbaum 847.782.1800

HIGHLAND PARK
Mrs. Michla Schanowitz 847.266.0770

NAPERVILLE
Rabbi Mendy Goldstein 630.957.8122

NORTHBROOK
Rabbi Meir Moscowitz 847.564.8770

NORWOOD PARK
Rabbi Mendel Perlstein 312.752.8894

OAK PARK
Rabbi Yitzchok Bergstein 708.524.1530

PEORIA
Rabbi Eli Langsam 309.370.7701

SKOKIE
Rabbi Yochanan Posner 847.677.1770

VERNON HILLS
Rabbi Shimmy Susskind 718.755.5356

WILMETTE
Rabbi Dovid Flinkenstein 847.251.7707

INDIANA

INDIANAPOLIS
Rabbi Avraham Grossbaum
Rabbi Dr. Shmuel Klatzkin 317.251.5573

IOWA

BETTENDORF
Rabbi Shneur Cadaner 563.355.1065

KANSAS

OVERLAND PARK
Rabbi Mendy Wineberg 913.649.4852

KENTUCKY

LOUISVILLE
Rabbi Avrohom Litvin 502.459.1770

LOUISIANA

BATON ROUGE
Rabbi Peretz Kazen 225.267.7047

METAIRIE
Rabbi Yossie Nemes
Rabbi Mendel Ceitlin 504.454.2910

NEW ORLEANS
Rabbi Mendel Rivkin 504.302.1830

MAINE

PORTLAND
Rabbi Levi Wilansky 207.650.1783

MARYLAND

BALTIMORE
Rabbi Velvel Belinsky 410.764.5000
Classes in Russian

Rabbi Dovid Reyder 781.796.4204

BEL AIR
Rabbi Kushi Schusterman 443.353.9718

BETHESDA
Rabbi Sender Geisinsky 301.913.9777

CHEVY CHASE
Rabbi Zalman Minkowitz 301.260.5000

COLUMBIA
Rabbi Hillel Baron
Rabbi Yosef Chaim Sufrin 410.740.2424

FREDERICK
Rabbi Boruch Labkowski 301.996.3659

GAITHERSBURG
Rabbi Sholom Raichik 301.926.3632

OLNEY
Rabbi Bentzy Stolik 301.660.6770

OWINGS MILLS
Rabbi Nochum Katsenelenbogen.....................410.356.5156

POTOMAC
Rabbi Mendel Bluming...................................301.983.4200
Rabbi Mendel Kaplan....................................301.983.1485

ROCKVILLE
Rabbi Shlomo Beitsh.....................................646.773.2675
Rabbi Moishe Kavka......................................301.836.1242

MASSACHUSETTS

ANDOVER
Rabbi Asher Bronstein...................................978.470.2288

ARLINGTON
Rabbi Avi Bukiet..617.909.8653

BOSTON
Rabbi Yosef Zaklos.......................................617.297.7282

BRIGHTON
Rabbi Dan Rodkin..617.787.2200

CAPE COD
Rabbi Yekusiel Alperowitz..............................508.775.2324

CHESTNUT HILL
Rabbi Mendy Uminer.....................................617.738.9770

LEXINGTON
Rabbi Yisroel New...646.248.9053

LONGMEADOW
Rabbi Yakov Wolff..413.567.8665

NEWTON
Rabbi Shalom Ber Prus..................................617.244.1200

PEABODY
Rabbi Nechemia Schusterman.........................978.977.9111

SUDBURY
Rabbi Yisroel Freeman...................................978.443.0110

SWAMPSCOTT
Rabbi Yossi Lipsker.......................................781.581.3833

MICHIGAN

ANN ARBOR
Rabbi Aharon Goldstein.................................734.995.3276

BLOOMFIELD HILLS
Rabbi Levi Dubov...248.949.6210

GRAND RAPIDS
Rabbi Mordechai Haller.................................616.957.0770

TROY
Rabbi Menachem Caytak................................248.873.5851

WEST BLOOMFIELD
Rabbi Shneur Silberberg................................248.855.6170

MINNESOTA

MINNETONKA
Rabbi Mordechai Grossbaum
Rabbi Shmuel Silberstein................................952.929.9922

S. PAUL
Rabbi Shneur Zalman Bendet...........................651.998.9298

MISSOURI

S. LOUIS
Rabbi Yosef Landa..314.725.0400
Rabbi Yosef Abenson.....................................314.448.0927

MONTANA

BOZEMAN
Rabbi Chaim Shaul Bruk................................406.600.4934

NEVADA

LAS VEGAS
Rabbi Yosef Rivkin..702.217.2170

SUMMERLIN
Rabbi Yisroel Schanowitz
Rabbi Tzvi Bronchtain....................................702.855.0770

NEW JERSEY

BASKING RIDGE
Rabbi Mendy Herson
Rabbi Mendel Shemtov...................................908.604.8844

CHERRY HILL
Rabbi Mendel Mangel....................................856.874.1500

CLINTON
Rabbi Eli Kornfeld 908.623.7000

ENGLEWOOD
Rabbi Shmuel Konikov 201.519.7343

FAIR LAWN
Rabbi Avrohom Bergstein 201.794.3770

GREATER MERCER COUNTY
Rabbi Dovid Dubov
Rabbi Yaakov Chaiton 609.213.4136

HASKELL
Rabbi Mendy Gurkov 201.696.7609

HOLMDEL
Rabbi Shmaya Galperin 732.772.1998

MADISON
Rabbi Shalom Lubin 973.377.0707

MANALAPAN
Rabbi Boruch Chazanow
Rabbi Levi Wolosow 732.972.3687

MEDFORD
Rabbi Yitzchok Kahan 609.451.3522

MOUNTAIN LAKES
Rabbi Levi Dubinsky 973.551.1898

MULLICA HILL
Rabbi Avrohom Richler 856.733.0770

OLD TAPPAN
Rabbi Mendy Lewis 201.767.4008

RED BANK
Rabbi Dovid Harrison 718.915.8748

ROCKAWAY
Rabbi Asher Herson
Rabbi Mordechai Baumgarten 973.625.1525

RUTHERFORD
Rabbi Yitzchok Lerman 347.834.7500

SCOTCH PLAINS
Rabbi Avrohom Blesofsky 908.790.0008

SHORT HILLS
Rabbi Mendel Solomon
Rabbi Avrohom Levin 973.725.7008

SOUTH BRUNSWICK
Rabbi Levi Azimov 732.398.9492

TENAFLY
Rabbi Mordechai Shain 201.871.1152

TOMS RIVER
Rabbi Moshe Gourarie 732.349.4199

WEST ORANGE
Rabbi Mendy Kasowitz 973.325.6311

WOODCLIFF LAKE
Rabbi Dov Drizin 201.476.0157

NEW MEXICO

LAS CRUCES
Rabbi Bery Schmukler 575.524.1330

NEW YORK

ALBANY
Rabbi Mordechai Rubin 518.368.7886

BAY SHORE
Rabbi Shimon Stillerman 631.913.8770

BEDFORD
Rabbi Arik Wolf 914.666.6065

BENSONHURST
Rabbi Avrohom Hertz 718.753.7768

BINGHAMTON
Mrs. Rivkah Slonim 607.797.0015

BRIGHTON BEACH
Rabbi Dovid Okonov 718.368.4490
Rabbi Moshe Winner 718.946.9833

BRONXVILLE
Rabbi Sruli Deitsch 917.755.0078

BROOKLYN
Rabbi Nissi Eber 347.677.2276
Rabbi Dovid Okonov 917.754.6942

BROOKVILLE
Rabbi Mendy Heber 516.626.0600

CEDARHURST
Rabbi Zalman Wolowik 516.295.2478

COMMACK
Rabbi Mendel Teldon 631.543.3343

DELMAR
Rabbi Zalman Simon 518.866.7658

DOBBS FERRY
Rabbi Benjy Silverman 914.693.6100

EAST HAMPTON
Rabbi Leibel Baumgarten
Rabbi Mendy Goldberg 631.329.5800

ELLENVILLE
Rabbi Shlomie Deren 845.647.4450

FOREST HILLS
Rabbi Yossi Mendelson 917.861.9726

GLEN OAKS
Rabbi Shmuel Nadler 347.388.7064

GREAT NECK
Rabbi Yoseph Geisinsky 516.487.4554

KINGSTON
Rabbi Yitzchok Hecht 845.334.9044

LARCHMONT
Rabbi Mendel Silberstein 914.834.4321

LITTLE NECK
Rabbi Eli Shifrin 718.423.1235

LONG BEACH
Rabbi Eli Goodman 516.574.3905

MANHASSET
Rabbi Mendel Paltiel 516.984.0701

MINEOLA
Rabbi Anchelle Perl 516.739.3636

MONTEBELLO
Rabbi Shmuel Gancz 845.746.1927

MELVILLE
Rabbi Yosef Raskin 631.276.4453

NEW HARTFORD
Rabbi Levi Charitonow 716.322.8692

NEW YORK
Rabbi Yakov Bankhalter 917.613.1678
Rabbi Berel Gurevitch 212.518.3122
Rabbi Daniel Kraus 917.294.5567
Rabbi Shmuel Metzger 212.758.3770

NYC TRIBECA
Rabbi Zalman Paris 212.566.6764

NYC UPPER EAST SIDE
Rabbi Uriel Vigler 212.369.7310

NYC WEST SIDE
Rabbi Shlomo Kugel 212.864.5010

OCEANSIDE
Rabbi Levi Gurkow 516.764.7385

OSSINING
Rabbi Dovid Labkowski 914.923.2522

OYSTER BAY
Rabbi Shmuel Lipszyc
Rabbi Shalom Lipszyc 347.853.9992

PARK SLOPE
Rabbi Menashe Wolf 347.957.1291

PORT WASHINGTON
Rabbi Shalom Paltiel 516.767.8672

PROSPECT HEIGHTS
Rabbi Mendy Hecht 347.622.3599

ROCHESTER
Rabbi Nechemia Vogel 585.271.0330

ROSLYN HEIGHTS
Rabbi Aaron Konikov 516.484.3500

SOUTHAMPTON
Rabbi Chaim Pape 917.627.4865

STATEN ISLAND
Rabbi Mendy Katzman 718.370.8953

STONY BROOK
Rabbi Shalom Ber Cohen 631.585.0521

SUFFERN
Rabbi Shmuel Gancz 845.368.1889

YORKTOWN HEIGHTS
Rabbi Yehuda Heber 914.962.1111

NORTH CAROLINA

CARY
Rabbi Yisroel Cotlar 919.651.9710

CHAPEL HILL
Rabbi Zalman Bluming 919.357.5904

CHARLOTTE
Rabbi Yossi Groner
Rabbi Shlomo Cohen 704.366.3984

GREENSBORO
Rabbi Yosef Plotkin 336.617.8120

RALEIGH
Rabbi Pinchas Herman
Rabbi Lev Cotlar 919.637.6950

WINSTON-SALEM
Rabbi Levi Gurevitz 336.756.9069

OHIO

BEACHWOOD
Rabbi Moshe Gancz 216.647.4884

CINCINNATI
Rabbi Yisroel Mangel 513.793.5200

COLUMBUS
Rabbi Yitzi Kaltmann 614.294.3296

DAYTON
Rabbi Nochum Mangel
Rabbi Shmuel Klatzkin 937.643.0770

OKLAHOMA

OKLAHOMA CITY
Rabbi Ovadia Goldman 405.524.4800

TULSA
Rabbi Yehuda Weg 918.492.4499

OREGON

PORTLAND
Rabbi Mordechai Wilhelm 503.977.9947

SALEM
Rabbi Avrohom Yitzchok Perlstein 503.383.9569

TIGARD
Rabbi Menachem Orenstein 971.329.6661

PENNSYLVANIA

AMBLER
Rabbi Shaya Deitsch 215.591.9310

BALA CYNWYD
Rabbi Shraga Sherman 610.660.9192

CLARKS SUMMIT
Rabbi Benny Rapoport 570.587.3300

DOYLESTOWN
Rabbi Mendel Prus 215.340.1303

GLEN MILLS
Rabbi Yehuda Gerber 484.620.4162

LAFAYETTE HILL
Rabbi Yisroel Kotlarsky 484.533.7009

LANCASTER
Rabbi Elazar Green 717.723.8783

LEWISBURG
Rabbi Yisroel Baumgarten 631.880.2801

MONROEVILLE
Rabbi Mendy Schapiro 412.372.1000

NEWTOWN
Rabbi Aryeh Weinstein 215.497.9925

PHILADELPHIA: CENTER CITY
Rabbi Yochonon Goldman 215.238.2100

PITTSBURGH
Rabbi Yisroel Altein .... 412.422.7300 EXT. 269

PITTSBURGH: SOUTH HILLS
Rabbi Mendy Rosenblum 412.278.3693

READING
Rabbi Yosef Lipsker 610.334.3218

RYDAL
Rabbi Zushe Gurevitz 267.536.5757

UNIVERSITY PARK
Rabbi Nosson Meretsky 814.863.4929

WYNNEWOOD
Rabbi Moishe Brennan 610.529.9011

PUERTO RICO

CAROLINA
Rabbi Mendel Zarchi 787.253.0894

RHODE ISLAND

WARWICK
Rabbi Yossi Laufer 401.884.7888

SOUTH CAROLINA

BLUFFTON
Rabbi Menachem Hertz 843.301.1819

COLUMBIA
Rabbi Hesh Epstein
Rabbi Levi Marrus 803.782.1831

GREENVILLE
Rabbi Leibel Kesselman 864.534.7739

TENNESSEE

KNOXVILLE
Rabbi Yossi Wilhelm 865.588.8584

MEMPHIS
Rabbi Levi Klein 901.754.0404

TEXAS

AUSTIN
Rabbi Mendy Levertov 512.905.2778

BELLAIRE
Rabbi Yossi Zaklikofsky 713.839.8887

CYPRESS
Rabbi Levi Marinovsky 832.651.6964

DALLAS
Rabbi Mendel Dubrawsky
Rabbi Moshe Naparstek 972.818.0770

EL PASO
Rabbi Levi Greenberg 347.678.9762

FORT WORTH
Rabbi Dov Mandel 817.263.7701

HOUSTON
Rabbi Dovid Goldstein
Rabbi Zally Lazarus 281.589.7188
Rabbi Moishe Traxler 713.774.0300

HOUSTON: RICE UNIVERSITY AREA
Rabbi Eliezer Lazaroff 713.522.2004

LEAGUE CITY
Rabbi Yitzchok Schmukler 281.724.1554

PLANO
Rabbi Eli Block 214.620.4083
Rabbi Mendel Block 972.596.8270

ROCKWALL
Rabbi Moshe Kalmenson 469.350.5735

ROUND ROCK
Rabbi Mendel Marasow 512.387.3171

S. ANTONIO
Rabbi Chaim Block
Rabbi Levi Teldon 210.492.1085
Rabbi Tal Shaul 210.877.4218

SOUTHLAKE
Rabbi Levi Gurevitch 817.451.1171

SUGAR LAND
Rabbi Mendel Feigenson 832.758.0685

THE WOODLANDS
Rabbi Mendel Blecher 281.865.7242

UTAH

PARK CITY
Rabbi Yehuda Steiger 435.714.8590

SALT LAKE CITY
Rabbi Benny Zippel 801.467.7777

S. GEORGE
Rabbi Mendy Cohen 862.812.6224

VERMONT

BURLINGTON
Rabbi Yitzchok Raskin 802.658.5770

VIRGINIA

ALEXANDRIA/ARLINGTON
Rabbi Mordechai Newman 703.370.2774

FAIRFAX
Rabbi Leibel Fajnland 703.426.1980

GAINESVILLE
Rabbi Shmuel Perlstein 571.445.0342

LOUDOUN COUNTY
Rabbi Chaim Cohen 248.298.9279

NORFOLK
Rabbi Aaron Margolin
Rabbi Levi Brashevitzky 757.616.0770

RICHMOND
Rabbi Shlomo Pereira 804.740.2000

WINCHESTER
Rabbi Yishai Dinerman 540.324.9879

WASHINGTON

BAINBRIDGE ISLAND
Rabbi Mendy Goldshmid 206.397.7679

BELLINGHAM
Rabbi Yosef Truxton 360.224.9919

MERCER ISLAND
Rabbi Elazar Bogomilsky 206.527.1411
Rabbi Nissan Kornfeld 206.851.2324

OLYMPIA
Rabbi Yosef Schtroks 360.867.8804

SEATTLE
Rabbi Yoni Levitin 206.851.9831
Rabbi Shnai Levitin 347.342.2259

SPOKANE COUNTY
Rabbi Yisroel Hahn 509.443.0770

WISCONSIN

BAYSIDE
Rabbi Cheski Edelman 414.439.5041

BROOKFIELD
Rabbi Levi Brook 925.708.4203

KENOSHA
Rabbi Tzali Wilschanski 262.359.0770

MADISON
Rabbi Avremel Matusof 608.335.3777

MEQUON
Rabbi Menachem Rapoport 262.242.2235

MILWAUKEE
Rabbi Levi Emmer 414.277.8839
Rabbi Mendel Shmotkin 414.961.6100

ARGENTINA

BUENOS AIRES
Mrs. Chani Gorowitz 54.11.4865.0445
Rabbi Menachem M. Grunblatt 54.911.3574.0037
Rabbi Mendy Gurevitch 55.11.4545.7771
Rabbi Shlomo Levy 54.11.4807.2223
Rabbi Yosef Levy 54.11.4504.1908
Rabbi Mendi Mizrahi 54.11.4963.1221
Rabbi Shiele Plotka 54.11.4634.3111
Rabbi Pinhas Sudry 54.1.4822.2285
Rabbi Shloimi Setton 54.11.4982.8637

CORDOBA
Rabbi Menajem Turk 54.351.233.8250

SALTA
Rabbi Rafael Tawil 54.387.421.4947

S. MIGUEL DE TUCUMÁN
Rabbi Ariel Levy 54.381.473.6944

AUSTRALIA

NEW SOUTH WALES

BELLEVUE HILL
Mrs. Chaya Kaye 614.3342.2755

DOUBLE BAY
Rabbi Yanky Berger 612.9327.1644

DOVER HEIGHTS
Rabbi Motti Feldman 614.0400.8572

NEWTOWN
Rabbi Eli Feldman 614.0077.0613

NORTH SHORE
Rabbi Nochum Schapiro
Rebbetzin Fruma Schapiro 612.9488.9548

TASMANIA

SOUTH LAUNCESTON
Mrs. Rochel Gordon 614.2055.0405

QUEENSLAND

BRISBANE
Rabbi Levi Jaffe 617.3843.6770

VICTORIA

EAST S. KILDA
Rabbi Sholem Gorelik 614.5244.8770

MOORABBIN
Rabbi Elisha Greenbaum 614.0349.0434

WESTERN AUSTRALIA

PERTH
Rabbi Shalom White 618.9275.2106

AZERBAIJAN

BAKU
Mrs. Chavi Segal 994.12.597.91.90

BELARUS

BOBRUISK
Mrs. Mina Hababo 375.29.104.3230

MINSK
Rabbi Shneur Deitsch
Mrs. Bassie Deitsch 375.29.330.6675

BELGIUM

ANTWERP
Rabbi Mendel Gurary 32.48.656.9878

BRUSSELS
Rabbi Shmuel Pinson 375.29.330.6675

BRAZIL

CURITIBA
Rabbi Mendy Labkowski 55.41.3079.1338

S. PAULO
Rabbi Avraham Steinmetz 55.11.3081.3081

CANADA

ALBERTA

CALGARY
Rabbi Mordechai Groner 403.281.3770

EDMONTON
Rabbi Ari Drelich
Rabbi Mendy Blachman 780.200.5770

BRITISH COLUMBIA

NANAIMO
Rabbi Benzti Shemtov 250.797.7877

RICHMOND
Rabbi Yechiel Baitelman 604.277.6427

VANCOUVER
Rabbi Dovid Rosenfeld 604.266.1313
Rabbi Shmuel Yeshayahu 604.738.7060

VICTORIA
Rabbi Meir Kaplan 250.595.7656

MANITOBA

WINNIPEG
Rabbi Shmuel Altein 204.339.8737

ONTARIO

BAYVIEW
Rabbi Levi Gansburg 416.551.9391

MAPLE
Rabbi Yechezkel Deren 647.883.6372

MISSISSAUGA
Rabbi Yitzchok Slavin 905.820.4432

NORTH YORK
Rabbi Sruli Steiner 647.501.5618

OTTAWA
Rabbi Menachem M. Blum 613.843.7770

RICHMOND HILL
Rabbi Mendel Bernstein 905.303.1880

THORNHILL
Rabbi Yisroel Landa 416.897.3338

GREATER TORONTO REGIONAL OFFICE & THORNHILL
Rabbi Yossi Gansburg 905.731.7000

TORONTO
Rabbi Shmuel Neft 647.966.7105
Rabbi Moshe Steiner 416.635.9606

WATERLOO
Rabbi Moshe Goldman 226.338.7770

QUEBEC

CÔTE S.-LUC
Rabbi Levi Naparstek 438.409.6770

DOLLARD-DES ORMEAUX
Rabbi Leibel Fine 514.777.4675

HAMPSTEAD
Rabbi Moshe New
Rabbi Berel Bell 514.739.0770

MONTREAL
Rabbi Ronnie Fine
Pesach Nussbaum 514.738.3434

OLD MONTREAL/GRIFFINTOWN
Rabbi Nissan Gansbourg
Rabbi Berel Bell 514.800.6966

S. LAZARE
Rabbi Nochum Labkowski 514.436.7426

TOWN OF MOUNT ROYAL
Rabbi Moshe Krasnanski
Rabbi Shneur Zalman Rader 514.342.1770

SASKATCHEWAN

SASKATOON
Rabbi Raphael Kats 306.384.4370

CAYMAN ISLANDS

GEORGE TOWN
Rabbi Berel Pewzner 717.798.1040

COLOMBIA

BOGOTA
Rabbi Chanoch Piekarski 57.1.635.8251

COSTA RICA

S. JOSÉ
Rabbi Hershel Spalter
Rabbi Moshe Bitton 506.4010.1515

CROATIA

ZAGREB
Rabbi Pinchas Zaklas 385.1.4812227

DENMARK

COPENHAGEN
Rabbi Yitzchok Loewenthal 45.3316.1850

DOMINICAN REPUBLIC

S. DOMINGO
Rabbi Shimon Pelman 829.341.2770

ESTONIA

TALLINN
Rabbi Shmuel Kot 372.662.30.50

FRANCE

BOULOGNE
Rabbi Michael Sojcher 33.1.46.99.87.85

DIJON
Rabbi Chaim Slonim 33.6.52.05.26.65

LA VARENNE-S.-HILAIRE
Rabbi Mena'hem Mendel Benelbaz 33.6.17.81.57.47

MARSEILLE
Rabbi Eliahou Altabe 33.6.11.60.03.05
Rabbi Mena'hem Mendel Assouline 33.6.64.88.25.04
Rabbi Emmanuel Taubenblatt 33.4.88.00.94.85

PARIS
Rabbi Yona Hasky 33.1.53.75.36.01
Rabbi Acher Marciano 33.6.15.15.01.02
Rabbi Avraham Barou'h Pevzner 33.6.99.64.07.70

PONTAULT-COMBAULT
Rabbi Yossi Amar 33.6.61.36.07.70

VILLIERS-SUR-MARNE
Rabbi Mena'hem Mendel Mergui 33.1.49.30.89.66

GEORGIA

TBILISI
Rabbi Meir Kozlovsky 995.32.2429770

GERMANY

BERLIN
Rabbi Yehuda Tiechtel 49.30.2128.0830

DUSSELDORF
Rabbi Chaim Barkahn 49.173.2871.770

HAMBURG
Rabbi Shlomo Bistritzky 49.40.4142.4190

HANNOVER 49.511.811.2822
Chapter founded by Rabbi Binyamin Wolff, OBM

GREECE

ATHENS
Rabbi Mendel Hendel 30.210.323.3825

GUATEMALA

GUATEMALA CITY
Rabbi Shalom Pelman 502.2485.0770

ISRAEL

ASHKELON
Rabbi Shneor Lieberman 054.977.0512

BALFURYA
Rabbi Noam Bar-Tov 054.580.4770

CAESAREA
Rabbi Chaim Meir Lieberman 054.621.2586

EVEN YEHUDA
Rabbi Menachem Noyman 054.777.0707

GANEI TIKVA
Rabbi Gershon Shnur 054.524.2358

GIV'ATAYIM
Rabbi Pinchus Bitton 052.643.8770

JERUSALEM
Rabbi Levi Diamond 055.665.7702
Rabbi Avraham Hendel 054.830.5799

KARMIEL
Rabbi Mendy Elishevitz 054.521.3073

KFAR SABA
Rabbi Yossi Baitch 054.445.5020

KIRYAT BIALIK
Rabbi Pinny Marton 050.661.1768

KIRYAT MOTZKIN
Rabbi Shimon Eizenbach 050.902.0770

KOCHAV YAIR
Rabbi Dovi Greenberg 054.332.6244

MACCABIM-RE'UT
Rabbi Yosef Yitzchak Noiman 054.977.0549

NES ZIYONA
Rabbi Menachem Feldman 054.497.7092

NETANYA
Rabbi Schneur Brod 054.579.7572

RAMAT GAN-KRINITZI
Rabbi Yisroel Gurevitz 052.743.2814

RAMAT GAN-MAROM NAVE
Rabbi Binyamin Meir Kali 050.476.0770

RAMAT YISHAI
Rabbi Shneor Zalman Wolosow 052.324.5475

RISHON LEZION
Rabbi Uri Keshet 050.722.4593

ROSH PINA
Rabbi Sholom Ber Hertzel 052.458.7600

TEL AVIV
Rabbi Shneur Piekarski 054.971.5568

JAMAICA

MONTEGO BAY
Rabbi Yaakov Raskin 876.452.3223

JAPAN

TOKYO
Rabbi Mendi Sudakevich 81.3.5789.2846

KAZAKHSTAN

ALMATY
Rabbi Shevach Zlatopolsky 7.7272.77.59.49

KYRGYZSTAN

BISHKEK
Rabbi Arye Raichman 996.312.68.19.66

LATVIA

RIGA
Rabbi Shneur Zalman Kot
Mrs. Rivka Glazman 371.6720.40.22

LITHUANIA

VILNIUS
Rabbi Sholom Ber Krinsky 370.6817.1367

LUXEMBOURG

LUXEMBOURG
Rabbi Mendel Edelman 352.2877.7079

MEXICO

S. MIGUEL DE ALLENDE
Rabbi Daniel Huebner 52.41.5181.8092

NETHERLANDS

ALMERE
Rabbi Moshe Stiefel 31.36.744.0509

AMSTERDAM
Rabbi Yanki Jacobs 31.644.988.627
Rabbi Jaacov Zwi Spiero 31.652.328.065

EINDHOVEN
Rabbi Simcha Steinberg 31.63.635.7593

HAGUE
Rabbi Shmuel Katzman 31.70.347.0222

HEEMSTEDE-HAARLEM
Rabbi Shmuel Spiero 31.23.532.0707

MAASTRICHT
Rabbi Avrohom Cohen 32.48.549.6766

NIJMEGEN
Rabbi Menachem Mendel Levine 31.621.586.575

ROTTERDAM
Rabbi Yehuda Vorst 31.10.265.5530

PANAMA

PANAMA CITY
Rabbi Ari Laine
Rabbi Gabriel Benayon 507.223.3383

RUSSIA

ASTRAKHAN
Rabbi Yisroel Melamed 7.851.239.28.24

BRYANSK
Rabbi Menachem Mendel Zaklas 7.483.264.55.15

CHELYABINSK
Rabbi Meir Kirsh 7.351.263.24.68

MOSCOW
Rabbi Aizik Rosenfeld 7.906.762.88.81
Rabbi Mordechai Weisberg 7.495.645.50.00

NIZHNY NOVGOROD
Rabbi Shimon Bergman 7.920.253.47.70

NOVOSIBIRSK
Rabbi Shneur Zalmen Zaklos 7.903.900.43.22

OMSK
Rabbi Osher Krichevsky 7.381.231.33.07

PERM
Rabbi Zalman Deutch 7.342.212.47.32

ROSTOV
Rabbi Chaim Danzinger 7.8632.99.02.68

S. PETERSBURG
Rabbi Shalom Pewzner 7.911.726.21.19
Rabbi Zvi Pinsky 7.812.713.62.09

SAMARA
Rabbi Shlomo Deutch 7.846.333.40.64

SARATOV
Rabbi Yaakov Kubitshek 7.8452.21.58.00

TOGLIATTI
Rabbi Meier Fischer 7.848.273.02.84

UFA
Rabbi Dan Krichevsky 7.347.244.55.33

VORONEZH
Rabbi Levi Stiefel 7.473.252.96.99

SINGAPORE

SINGAPORE
Rabbi Mordechai Abergel 656.337.2189
Rabbi Netanel Rivni 656.336.2127
Classes in Hebrew

SOUTH AFRICA

JOHANNESBURG
Rabbi Dovid Masinter
Rabbi Ari Kievman 27.11.440.6600

SWEDEN

STOCKHOLM
Rabbi Chaim Greisman 46.70.790.8994

SWITZERLAND

LUZERN
Rabbi Chaim Drukman 41.41.361.1770

THAILAND

BANGKOK
Rabbi Yosef C. Kantor 6681.837.7618

UKRAINE

BERDITCHEV
Mrs. Chana Thaler 380.637.70.37.70

DNEPROPETROVSK
Rabbi Dan Makagon 380.504.51.13.18

NIKOLAYEV
Rabbi Sholom Gotlieb 380.512.37.37.71

ODESSA
Rabbi Avraham Wolf
Rabbi Yaakov Neiman 38.048.728.0770 EXT. 280

ZAPOROZHYE
Mrs. Nechama Dina Ehrentreu 380.957.19.96.08

ZHITOMIR
Rabbi Shlomo Wilhelm 380.504.63.01.32

UNITED KINGDOM

BOURNEMOUTH
Rabbi Bentzion Alperowitz 44.749.456.7177

CHEADLE
Rabbi Peretz Chein 44.161.428.1818

ESSEX

EPPING
Rabbi Yossi Posen 44.749.650.4345

LEEDS
Rabbi Eli Pink 44.113.266.3311

LONDON
Rabbi Moshe Adler 44.771.052.4460
Rabbi Boruch Altein 44.749.612.3342
Rabbi Mechel Gancz 44.758.332.3074
Rabbi Chaim Hoch 44.753.879.9524
Rabbi Dovid Katz 44.207.625.2682
Mrs. Esther Kesselman 44.794.432.4829
Rabbi Mendy Korer 44.794.632.5444
Rabbi Eli Levin 44.754.046.1568
Mrs. Chanie Simon 44.208.458.0416
Rabbi Bentzi Sudak 44.781.211.1890
Rabbi Shneur Wineberg 44.745.628.6538

MANCHESTER
Rabbi Levi Cohen 44.161.792.6335
Rabbi Shmuli Jaffe 44.161.766.1812

RADLETT, HERTFORDSHIRE
Rabbi Alexander Sender Dubrawsky 44.794.380.8965

JEWISH LEARNING INSTITUTE

The Jewish Learning Multiplex

Brought to you by the Rohr Jewish Learning Institute

In fulfillment of the mandate of the Lubavitcher Rebbe, of blessed memory, whose leadership guides every step of our work, the mission of the Rohr Jewish Learning Institute is to transform Jewish life and the greater community through the study of Torah, connecting each Jew to our shared heritage of Jewish learning.

While our flagship program remains the cornerstone of our organization, JLI is proud to feature additional divisions catering to specific populations, in order to meet a wide array of educational needs.

THE ROHR JEWISH LEARNING INSTITUTE

A subsidiary of Merkos L'Inyonei Chinuch,
the adult educational arm of the Chabad-Lubavitch movement

Torah Studies provides a rich and nuanced encounter with the weekly Torah reading.

Jewish teens forge their identity as they engage in Torah study, social interaction, and serious fun.

The **Rosh Chodesh Society** gathers Jewish women together once a month for intensive textual study.

TorahCafe.com provides an exclusive selection of top-rated Jewish educational videos.

Participants delve into our nation's past while exploring the Holy Land's relevance and meaning today.

This yearly event rejuvenates mind, body, and spirit with a powerful synthesis of Jewish learning and community.

Equips youths facing adulthood with education and resources to address youth mental health.

Select affiliates are invited to partner with peers and noted professionals, as leaders of innovation and excellence.

MyShiur courses are designed to assist students in developing the skills needed to study Talmud independently.

This rigorous fellowship program invites select college students to explore the fundamentals of Judaism.

A crash course that teaches adults to read Hebrew in just five sessions.

Machon Shmuel is an institute providing Torah research in the service of educators worldwide.

Notes

Envy Dakota in Schan
Caliente in blobs Btress   33e2442a

Reve Dakota icedb
  R Ocean R613B614   1488M
          R1226CHM *   sandy b rooted

Est Blonds R26613 Deena
  Finn 1488R
  India Ruff
  RonA
_____
*[Luna EW   ellanila.com
Sandra   Oasis Nails
Shelton J Festival
  364-4149
Joslyn Rof P notsure
_____
Gabor. Delatoit i chap. blonde
Emelia Jr long bob (nah)